FOOD · FOR · THOUGHT

FOOD · FOR · THOUGHT

HEALING THE MIND, BODY & SOUL

A COOKBOOK WITH RECIPES SUBMITTED
BY THE CONSUMER ADVISORY BOARD OF THE
COMMUNICABLE DISEASE PREVENTION PROGRAM (CDPP)
OF CODMAN SQUARE HEALTH CENTER

DISCLAIMER

This book is written as a source of information only. The information in this book should by no means be considered a substitute for the advice of a qualified medical professional, who should always be consulted before beginning any new diet or other health program.

Members of Codman Square Health Center's (Codman or CSHC or Health Center) Communicable Disease Prevention Program (CDPP) Consumer Advisory Board shared these recipes with cookbook readers. Codman Square Health Center's Nutrition staff have reviewed the recipes. Codman Square Health Center is not responsible for the outcome of any of the recipes included in this book. The authors, editor, and publisher expressly disclaim responsibility for any adverse effects arising from the use or application of the information contained herein.

NUTRITION NOTE

The orange notes in the recipe margins are tips to make the recipes healthier. They mainly focus on reducing total calories, sodium, and saturated fat without significantly altering the flavor profile of the original recipe.

Codman Square Health Center

© 2021 Codman Square Health Center

Codman Square Health Center, 637 Washington St., Dorchester, MA 02124
(617) 825-9660 • www.codman.org

CONTRIBUTORS

The Codman Square Health Center Communicable Disease Prevention Program (CDPP) Consumer Advisory Board (also known as the CAB) is a voluntary group of Codman Square community members and CSHC patients, who serve in an advisory capacity for the Health Center and for the services provided in the CDPP department. CAB members are enthusiastic about affecting change and improving the livelihoods of People Living with HIV/AIDS (PLWH), as well as all individuals accessing health care through CSHC and beyond.

PROJECT MANAGER
Harvard Thompson, MPH

NUTRITIONAL CONSULTANT
Kathy Ireland, MS, RDN, LDN

LAYOUT AND DESIGN
Daniel Goodwin

EDITORIAL TEAM
John Galluzzo
Daniel Goodwin
Kathy Ireland
Christine Leccese
Harvard Thompson

SPONSOR
Boston Public Health Commission

CONTRIBUTORS
- CDPP staff:
  Jonathan Pincus, MD
  Jahna Knobler, NP
  Maureen Scott, NP
  Florence Oknokwo, RN
  Carole Brignol
  Carla Kenneally
  Nurukisutu Nabbumba
  Tatiana Torres
  Lesly Ovilmar
  Gregory Jean-Louis
  Emir Duhovic
  Valerie Austin
  Matthew Spence
  Maeva Veillard
  Stephane Victor
  De'Zyre Lewis
  Cherish Lamar-Smith
  Tai Tran
- CDPP Consumer Advisory Board
- CDPP consumers

Food for Thought: Healing the Mind, Body & Soul is published by The Codman Square Health Center. Learn more about our health and community services at codman.org

Contents

Thank you ...

... to Codman Square Health Center

... to the Codman Square Health Center
Consumer Advisory Board

... to the Codman Square and
Dorchester community

... to the brothers, sisters, mothers, fathers, aunts,
uncles, grandparents, friends, strangers and
beyond who have been diagnosed with HIV

... to those who have died
of HIV/AIDS-related complications

A global effort

This year we commemorate 40 years since the first five reported cases of HIV/AIDS in the U.S., as we enter the second year of a new global pandemic — COVID-19. The lessons we learned through the decades of fighting HIV helped inform efforts to control the spread of COVID-19.

We mourn the loss of more than 35 million people to AIDS, while also celebrating their lives and contributions and the progress of those currently living with HIV. We continue to be committed to ending the HIV pandemic and related stigma.

The HIV pandemic highlighted the effects of insufficient access to care, global disparities in health care, structural racism and homophobia, the importance of social determinants of health, the benefits of harm reduction, and the tragic consequences of stigma and scapegoating. A global effort of activists, scientists, public health officials, and health care personnel helped to make progress on these issues. While there is still much work to be done, HIV is now a treatable chronic condition and global access to care, while not ideal, is better than for almost any other illness.

People living with HIV/AIDS and activists who courageously shared their stories and advocated for a seat at the table have driven this process since the beginning. They advocated for faster progress in everything from basic science and drug approval to clinical and public health funding.

The voices of people living with HIV/AIDS, their dedication, advocacy, and bravery have been an historic force in the progress and response to the HIV pandemic. This cookbook celebrates the diversity, advocacy, lives, and personal stories of some of these individuals. Food is not only a necessity of life, but a window into the diversity of our lives, and a vehicle for sharing our resources and humanity.

Thank you to those who have helped shape the response to the HIV pandemic and who have shared their recipes and their stories. I am humbled by your dedication and advocacy.

Jonathan Pincus, MD
Clinical Director, HIV, Hepatitis C, and STD clinical programs,
Codman Square Health Center

Everybody EATS!

Dear readers,

Over the course of the past six months, members of the Codman Square Health Center (CSHC) Consumer Advisory Board (CAB) have poured their hearts and souls into this cookbook with the goal of uniting the community in a shared love of food. Food sustains us and can unite us. Quite simply, everybody eats.

However, everyone does not have equal access to food — socio-economic disparities often result in food insecurity.[1] In Suffolk County, Massachusetts, (which includes Dorchester and other Boston-based communities), one in 13 people were at risk of hunger prior to the COVID-19 pandemic. Since the pandemic began, one in 8 people are at risk of or facing hunger.[2]

While economic relief from the government, community-based organizations, and other efforts have helped, there is still a lot we need to do to address food insecurity. Social Determinants of Health (SDoH), such as access to health care, childcare, transportation, affordable food, and employment remain ongoing barriers that can stimy positive outcomes.

Nevertheless, food is something that connects us, transcends culture, and unites individuals and families. After all, what culture doesn't get together to celebrate, grieve, and connect with food? That is why we decided to make a cookbook — to share the recipes that bring people together.

Our goals for this cookbook include demonstrating how food has the potential to brighten a person's and a family's day. It is the thoughtfulness, care, and intention behind each recipe that matters. It is also the stories, traditions, and familial bonds that bring recipes to life. Food is a language that requires no words, only that the person eating the food be present.

When we come to the table, we break bread as a family. Regardless of whether those at the table share blood. Going back hundreds of generations, sharing a meal has been a sign of peace, a reconciliation, and a welcoming. There is no better time for us to come together and love one another, and ourselves, for together we are stronger than we are alone.

Part of the joy of developing this cookbook, with the guidance of the CAB, has been that I have had the pleasure of hearing the stories and traditions behind each recipe. If only I could translate the emotions of those conversations into words, so that every reader could appreciate the pride and love that is associated with cooking. I hope you can feel it when you read about and prepare the recipes in this book.

For many, cooking is an act of self-care — it is an opportunity for people to let their edible ensembles tell a story. Some people cook because they enjoy making others happy. Whatever the reason, be assured that each of the recipes in this cookbook come with a story.

HIV/AIDS Education

Another goal of this cookbook is to educate readers about HIV/AIDS, which is a public health crisis for the world, and especially in our community of Dorchester, Massachusetts. With this cookbook, we hope to provide insight into the *Human Immunodeficiency Virus (HIV)* and *Acquired Immuno-*

deficiency Syndrome (AIDS), and help readers to understand, appreciate, and respect it. We intend to break down many of the misconceptions surrounding HIV/AIDS by providing thorough education on it, including modes of transmission and prevention, and the ways in which a person can verify if they are HIV positive or not.

More than providing education on HIV/AIDS, our intention is to explain what it means to live with HIV — for persons who are HIV positive, also referred to as Persons Living with HIV (PLWH). With advances in medicine, PLWH can live full, healthy lives, without fear of dying from HIV/AIDS. According to the CDC (2014), the average lifespan of PLWH is about 71 years.[3] This alone is cause for celebration!

HIV care, including access to medical providers, medicine, support staff, and resources for social determinants of health needs have enabled people living with HIV (PLWH) to live their lives to the fullest without the medical and financial barriers that once existed. At the Federal level, the Ryan White Cares Act, which was initially enacted by Congress in 1990, remains the largest federal-based program dedicated to providing HIV care and treatment services to PLWH, especially those who are uninsured and/or underserved.[4] At the local level, hospitals, community health centers, and community-based organizations who hire culturally competent staff to provide essential, hands-on support for PLWH to access essential HIV services and care has had a big impact on PLWH.

Recognizing how far we have come since HIV was first broadly known to the United States,[5] motivates us to continue the fight until HIV/AIDs is a topic of the past.

We need everyone's support to get to that point. As a community, we can start by destigmatizing HIV/AIDS and taking steps to prevent it.

We can do this by talking openly about getting regular health screenings and asking our healthcare providers about HIV tests. We can talk about sex with our children and let them know that they are in control of their future. We can mentor youth and those most vulnerable. We can be open to discussing topics that may be uncomfortable. The change we seek in our communities starts with us. We can do this, one step at a time.

Paying tribute

As we move forward, we must also pay tribute to those who came before us. In the fight against HIV/AIDS, we owe the progress we celebrate today to those we have lost to AIDS, and to the advocates who fought for acceptance, inclusion, and transparency. We owe it to our brothers, sisters, parents, children, and friends identifying as LGBTQIA+ who have been disproportionately affected by HIV/AIDS. Among many, a few notable advocacy initiatives for PLWH and HIV/AIDS include the 1987 AIDS Memorial Quilt,[6] the 2015 Surviving Voices initiative,[7] and AIDS Coalition to Unleash Power (ACT UP).[8]

Let our cookbook follow in those steps. We aspire to raise awareness and increase education for HIV/AIDS, while reducing stigma, fear, and misinformation. Most importantly, we seek to offer everyone a seat at our table, for good food, dialogue, and a promise for a brighter future.

Our wish is that we build a stronger youth and community-led coalition that roots out stigma and openly discusses the risks our communities face with HIV/AIDS. We only hope that one day we can look back upon the HIV/AIDS epidemic and say that we persevered.

So, the next time you enjoy one of these meals, please give thanks to those who came before, and for those we have lost along the way. Most importantly, please help pave the road to a tomorrow without HIV/AIDS.

With most gratitude,

Harvard Thompson
Manager, Communicable Disease Prevention Program,
Codman Square Health Center

THE COMMUNICABLE DISEASE PREVENTION PROGRAM (CDPP) IS THE CENTER OF SEXUAL HEALTH SERVICES, INCLUDING HIV (ALSO KNOWN AS THE RYAN WHITE HIV/AIDS PROGRAM), X-CLINIC (OUR STD TESTING AND TREATMENT CLINIC) AND THE EDUCATION AND OUTREACH TEAM, WHICH SUPPORTS COMMUNITY-WIDE HEALTH EDUCATION INITIATIVES, AT CODMAN SQUARE HEALTH CENTER.

1
Soups

FROM HEARTY TO CHEESEY TO RICH IN VEGETABLES, THESE BOWLS OF GOODNESS WILL FILL YOUR BELLY AND WARM YOUR HEART.

Broccoli Cheddar Soup

Our submitted Broccoli Cheddar Soup recipe allows for variation based on personal taste. If you like a chunkier soup, with more texture, add some extra broccoli.

This recipe is high in saturated fat, which is not great for heart health. Pick and choose from the suggestions below to lower the saturated fat in this soup without sacrificing flavor.

Switch out some or all of the butter for olive oil.

Try whole milk instead. To make it even healthier, use 1% or 2% milk.

Use reduced-sodium broth to lower salt content.

Try reduced-fat cheese instead.

INGREDIENTS

½	onion, chopped
2	ounces butter
1	cup shredded carrots
¼	cup flour
2	cups half & half
2	cups vegetable or chicken stock
2–3	cups of chopped broccoli
1–2	cups of cheddar cheese (shredded)

DIRECTIONS

Melt 2 ounces of butter (a half stick) in a pot with the onions and carrots. Cook on medium for 3-5 minutes until the vegetables start to soften.

Stir in the flour and then whisk in the half & half.

Add the 2 cups of stock and then add the broccoli. Let the mixture simmer for 25-30 minutes until the veggies are tender.

Add cheddar cheese. Allow it to melt for 5-10 minutes.

Soup Joumou

Also known as Haitian Squash Soup, this dish is more than just a meal; it's a statement in celebration of freedom. Serve it at any time of year, but know that if you do so on January 1st you are joining a cultural tradition shared by Haitians around the world remembering the revolution that emancipated their ancestors from slavery. "Squash" can be interpreted as butternut squash, pumpkin, or even sweet potatoes, based on availability and your palate. And this is your chance to try mirliton, or chayote, an edible member of the gourd family that was among the first plants shipped back to Europe from the New World during the 15th and 16th centuries.

Use low-sodium chicken broth to make this recipe a bit more heart-healthy.

Try whole-wheat pasta for added fiber.

INGREDIENTS

1	pound of beef, bone-in (can also use cubed)
1	liter chicken broth
2	cloves garlic, minced
2	tbsp olive oil
1	butternut squash (about 2½ to 3 pounds)
2	cups chopped celery
1	cup of fresh vegetables (potato, carrots, turnips, mirliton)
1	small cabbage, chopped
1	whole hot pepper
3	cups pasta (try penne or spaghetti, or both)
	Lemon juice/lemon zest from one lemon

DIRECTIONS

Marinate the beef with four spices. Try your own combination of salt, pepper, sage, ginger, and cloves.

In a pot, cook marinated meat for 30-40 minutes in 1 cup chicken broth, salt, pepper, minced garlic, and 1 tbsp olive oil until well-cooked.

In a separate pot, add remaining chicken broth, cut squash, 1 cup celery, garlic, sugar, salt, and pepper. Cook for 30 minutes. In a blender, mix these ingredients until you obtain a smooth mixture. Use a strainer to extract a very smooth squash juice.

Add mixture in a pot with diced vegetables, cabbage, cooked meat, lemon juice, whole hot pepper, bouquet garni, and pasta last.

Cook all for at least 30-40 minutes. Remove bouquet garni. Enjoy!

BOUQUET GARNI:

THE BOUQUET GARNI IS A BUNDLE OF HERBS USUALLY TIED TOGETHER WITH STRING AND MAINLY USED TO PREPARE SOUP, STOCK, AND STEWS. THE BOUQUET IS COOKED WITH THE OTHER INGREDIENTS, BUT IS REMOVED PRIOR TO CONSUMPTION.

HERBS & SPICES

Bouquet Garni
   (thyme, laurel, rosemary)

Salt

Black/white pepper

Sugar

Sage

Ginger

Cloves

Potage aux Legumes

We present a hearty French vegetable soup that goes well with the overall ambiance of the fall and winter months, helping to push the chill out of your bones. This soup is enjoyed best with friends and family, and perhaps a glass of white wine. Serve it hot and make sure to include your favorite crusty bread (a traditional French baguette is preferred). *Bon Appetit!*

Choose low or reduced-sodium stock to reduce salt intake

Try milk instead

Reduce to 1 tbsp. to lower the overall sodium in this recipe

INGREDIENTS

1	large golden beet
1	large parsnip
1	large potato
1	onion
4	carrots
4	pieces of celery
3	garlic cloves
2	tbsp. olive oil
½	cup white cooking wine
1	tbsp. salt
2½	cups of vegetable (or chicken) stock
¼	cup of heavy cream
2	tbsp. of butter

DIRECTIONS

Chop beet, parsnip, and potato into 1-inch cubes. Slice onions thinly and cut carrots and celery into 1-inch slices. Smash garlic cloves.

Heat olive oil in a pot, over medium heat, adding beets, parsnips, potato and ½ tbsp. of salt. Cover, cook for 10 minutes, stirring occasionally.

Add carrots, onions, and ½ tbsp. of salt. Cook another 5 minutes, stirring occasionally. Add celery, garlic and cook another 5 minutes, stirring occasionally.

Add wine to the pot, cook an additional 3 minutes, stirring occasionally. Add broth, slowly, stirring as you go.

Bring ingredients to a boil. Cover, reduce heat to low, and simmer for 20 to 25 minutes.

When vegetables are tender (test them with a fork), remove pot from heat. Add ingredients to a food processor and blend until all ingredients are smooth and creamy in consistency.

Add ¼ cup of heavy cream and 2 tbsp. of butter to the soup, stirring to blend.

Dish out into bowls, garnish and serve hot with crusty bread for dipping. Garnish as desired with parmesan cheese, chopped chives, salt and pepper.

Healthy Tips: **The DASH Diet**

WHAT IS THE DASH DIET?

DASH stands for "Dietary Approaches to Stop Hypertension." Hypertension, or high blood pressure, is dangerous because it makes your heart work too hard.

The DASH plan is a diet that is good for your heart. It focuses on foods that are high in fiber and vitamins and low in saturated fats, sugars, and sodium.

The DASH plan requires no special foods or recipes and can fit with many dierent individual preferences.

BASIC GUIDELINES OF THE DASH DIET

- **Focus on fiber by eating more fruits, vegetables, and whole grain foods:** these foods are naturally high in fiber and minerals and low in fat and sodium.

- **Choose more unsaturated fats and less saturated and trans fats:** Snack on nuts or seeds (unsaturated fat), and choose lean meats and low-fat dairy products (low saturated fat)

- **Reduce added sodium in your food:** Limit processed foods and condiments, and avoid using a salt shaker at the table.

- **Beware of added sugar:** instead of choosing candy for a snack or jelly for your toast, try a piece or fruit or peanut butter instead.

- **Exercise!** Try to be active at least 60 minutes on most days of the week

- **Reduce alcohol intake**

SAMPLE DASH MEAL PLANS

DAY 1	
BREAKFAST	1 cup oatmeal with skim & a banana 6 oz light vanilla yogurt with berries 6 oz orange juice
LUNCH	1 cup homemade vegetable and barley soup 2 slices whole grain bread with maragarine 1 cup diced mango or papaya 1 cup skim milk
A.M. SNACK	1 cup baby carrots with low-fat dip/dressing
DINNER	6 oz broiled fish with lemon Collard greens, sauteed in oil w/ onion & garlic ½ cup yams ½ cup brown rice with beans Water with lemon or lime
P.M. SNACK	5-6 whole grain crackers 1-2 oz low-fat cheese
DAY 2	
BREAKFAST	1 cup whole grain cereal (Wheaties™, Cheerios™, Raisin Bran™, etc.) with ½ cup skim milk 1 orange Coffee with low-fat milk or creamer
LUNCH	Turkey (2-3 slices) and low-fat cheese (1 slice) sandwich on whole grain bread 1 small salad with low-fat, low-sodium dressing 1 apple Water with lemon or lime
A.M. SNACK	¼ cup unsalted almonds ¼ cup dried fruit
DINNER	3-6 oz baked chicken breast ½ cup roasted red potatoes 1-2 cups broccoli and cauliflower medley Small dinner roll 1 cup skim milk
P.M. SNACK	1 cup low-fat frozen yogurt topped with berries 1 cup carrots and celery with hummus

HOW TO EAT ON THE DASH DIET

	#OF SERVINGS PER DAY	WHAT IS 1 SERVING?	DASH-APPROVED CHOICES	THINGS TO AVOID	TIPS
VEGETABLES	4-5	1 cup of leafy vegetables or ½ cup of raw or cooked vegetables	All vegetables are DASH-approved!	Packaged vegetables in sauce, as these often have a high sodium content	Rinse canned vegetables under cold water to remove excess salt
FRUITS	4	1 medium fruit, ½ cup fresh fruit, ¼ cup dried fruit	All fruits are DASH-approved!	Packaged vegetables in sauce, as these often have a high sodium content	Rinse canned fruits under cold water to remove excess sugar
WHOLE GRAIN	6-8	1 slice of bread or ½ cup of rice or pasta	Whole grain bread or pasta; brown rice; oatmeal	Limit white bread, white rice, and plain pasta	Make ½ of your daily grains choices whole grains
DAIRY FOODS	2-3	8 oz milk or yogurt; 1½ oz cheese	Fat free (skim) or low-fat (1%) milk, cheese, or yogurt	Full-fat (whole) milk, cheese, or yogurt; flavored milks and yogurts	Watch out for flavored milks and yogurts! They have a lot of added sugar
MEATS, POULTRY & FISH	1-2	3 oz (about the size of a deck of cards)	Fish rich in healthy fats (mackerel, salmon, tuna), all other fish, chicken, turkey; lean cuts of meat with fat removed; Meats that are broiled, roasted, or grilled	Red meat, fried meats, cured meats (bacon, deli meat); skin on poultry	Processed meat (deli meat, bacon) contains a lot of sodium and fat
NUTS, SEEDS & DRY BEANS	4-5 per week	⅓ cup nuts; 2 tablespoons of seeds; ½ cup beans	Almonds, mixed nuts, peanuts, walnuts, sunflower seeds, kidney beans	Salted nuts or seeds; canned beans with added salt	Try having a handful of nuts as a snack, or adding seeds to a salad!
FATS & OIL	2	1 teaspoon margarine or oil; 2 tablespoons salad dressing	Vegetable oils, soft margarine, low-fat mayonnaise, light salad dressings,	Butter, creamy salad dressings	Choose low-fat, low-sodium dressings or sauces, or try making your own!
SWEETS	2 per week	1 tablespoon sugar or jelly, 8 oz sugary beverage	1 or 2 sweets per week is okay on the DASH-diet	Candy, sugar, jelly or jam, fruit drinks, regular soda, ice cream, baked goods	Enjoy sweets in very limited amounts!

An introduction to HIV/AIDS

HIV Defined

The Human Immunodeficiency Virus (HIV) is a virus that targets the immune system. Once it has been established in the human body, it begins to replicate rapidly, which results in an increase "viral load." The higher the viral load a person has, the higher the possibility that HIV can be transmitted to another person (more on modes of transmission in the next chapter).

There are two main stages of HIV, including:

1) ACUTE

Acute HIV infection occurs within the first 2 to 4 weeks after exposure to HIV. This process is referred to as seroconverting—which means that the body produces antibodies in response to an antigen, and thus the HIV virus can be detected during blood tests screening for the virus. A person may experience flu-like symptoms during this process such as fever, chills, rash, muscle aches, fatigue, etc., though some people do not feel any symptoms at all. The symptoms are the body's reaction to the infection. During the acute phase, a person typically has a high viral load, and can be very contagious.

POSSIBLE SYMPTOMS DURING ACUTE HIV INFECTION:

- FEVER
- CHILLS
- RASH
- MUSCLE ACHES
- FATIGUE

2) CHRONIC

Chronic HIV infection is often an asymptomatic period for Persons Living with HIV (PLWH). At this point, the virus is replicating slower than it did during the acute phase. PLWH may not know they are HIV positive, without diagnosis through blood tests, and they can transmit HIV during this phase without medication intervention. The chronic phase can last up to a decade or more, and during this time, the viral load will continue to rise and the T lymphocytes (white blood cells, which fight off infection, also known as CD4 cells) decrease. As this occurs, a person may begin to experience the same flu-like symptoms described for acute infection.

IF A PERSON IS AWARE OF THEIR POSITIVE STATUS, THEN THEY CAN TAKE MEDICATION (ANTIRETROVIRALS, WHICH WILL BE DISCUSSED LATER IN THIS BOOK), TO PREVENT THE TRANSMISSION OF HIV TO OTHERS.

2–4 weeks

THE ACUTE STAGE OF HIV INFECTION OCCURS WITHIN THE FIRST 2–4 WEEKS AFTER EXPOSURE.

10 years

THE CHRONIC STAGE OF HIV INFECTION CAN LAST UP TO A DECADE OR MORE.

3 years

THE AVERAGE LIFESPAN OF A PERSON WITH AIDS, WITHOUT TREATMENT, IS ABOUT THREE YEARS.

If HIV is not treated (more on treatment in a following chapter, *Entrées*), it can lead to AIDS.

AIDS Defined

The Acquired Immunodeficiency Syndrome, also known as *AIDS,* is considered the third stage of HIV infection. AIDS occurs when a person has a high viral load and a reduced CD4 count (defined as 200 cells/mm). Persons with AIDS are highly susceptible to opportunistic infections, which can cause serious harm, even death. The average life span of a persons with AIDS, without treatment,[1] is about three years.

Demystifying the virus

First and foremost, HIV is treatable!

While there is currently no cure for HIV, with proper medical treatment, Including medication, PLWH can live a perfectly healthy, normal, and long life. Thanks to medical advances in medication and treatment, HIV is now considered a chronic condition, just like many other chronic conditions. Many PLWH may never progress into the third stage, known as AIDS.

The only way to verify if a person has HIV is through blood tests. It is recommended that all persons who are sexually active be routinely screened for HIV and other sexually transmitted infections *(STI)*. It is best to be screened at least once annually, or more frequently if a person has multiple sexual partners.

HIV can affect anyone — women, men, children, grandparents, cousins, sisters, brothers, friends, politicians, actors, athletes, journalists, etc. Since we are all at risk, we should all know about HIV so we can protect ourselves and provide love and support to PLWH in our lives and communities.

Keep in mind that PLWH cannot transmit through communicable interactions, such as playing sports, hugging, sharing utensils, holding hands, etc. HIV can only be transmitted through blood, semen, vaginal fluids and/or mother-to-child via uterine development and/or breastfeeding—more on this in the next chapter.

REFERENCE

About HIV/AIDS. CDC (2021). About HIV/AIDS | HIV Basics | HIV/AIDS | CDC. [ONLINE] Available at: https://www.cdc.gov/hiv/basics/whatishiv.html. [Accessed 23 March 2021].

OPPORTUNISTIC INFECTIONS

SOME OPPORTUNISTIC INFECTIONS THAT PEOPLE LIVING WITH AIDS ARE SUSCEPTIBLE TO ARE:

- **KAPOSI'S SARCOMA (KS)** — A VIRUS CAUSING PINK OR PURPLE SPOTS TO APPEAR ON THE SKIN; IT CAN BE FATAL IF IT SPREADS TO LUNGS OR LYMPH NODES

- **PNEUMONIA** — AN INFECTION OF ONE OR BOTH OF THE LUNGS, WHICH CAUSES DIFFICULTY BREATHING, INCLUDING FEVER, COUGH, AND FOR PERSONS WITH A WEAKENED IMMUNE SYSTEM, CAN BE FATAL

- **WASTING SYNDROME** — DEFINED AS AN INVOLUNTARY LOSS OF MORE THAN 10 PERCENT OF BODY MASS, WHILE EXPERIENCING DIARRHEA, WEAKNESS, FEVER (CDC, 2021).

REFERENCE

Centers for Disease Control and Prevention (CDC). (2021). AIDS and Opportunistic Infections [Online]. Available at: https://www.cdc.gov/hiv/basics/livingwithhiv/opportunisticinfections.html (Accessed: 23 April 2021).

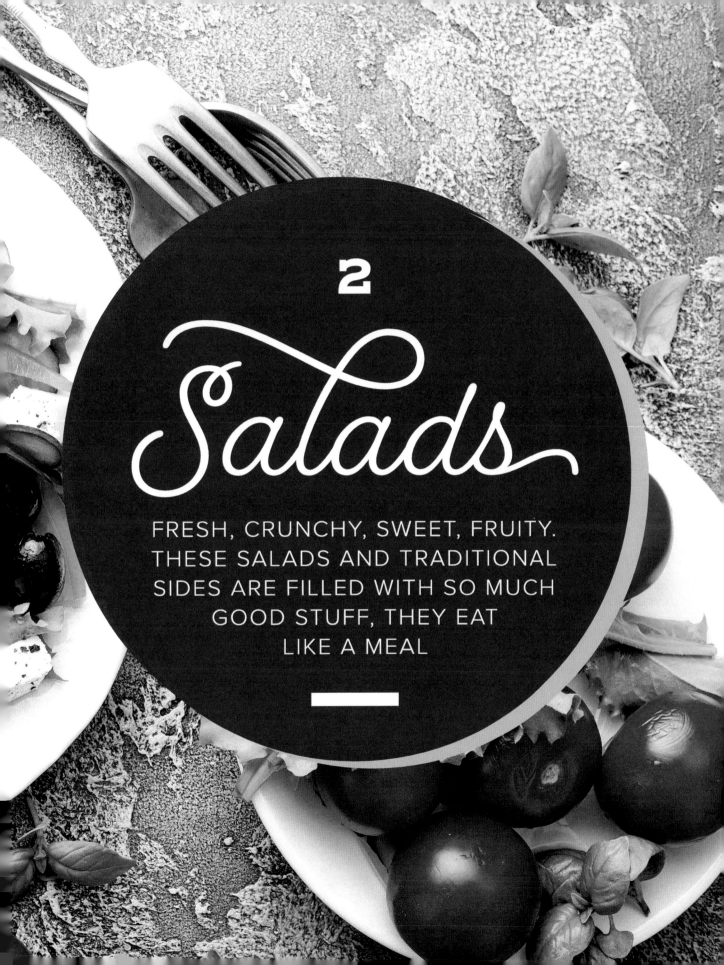

2

Salads

FRESH, CRUNCHY, SWEET, FRUITY.
THESE SALADS AND TRADITIONAL
SIDES ARE FILLED WITH SO MUCH
GOOD STUFF, THEY EAT
LIKE A MEAL

Spring Lettuce Salad

Sometimes a salad is all we need to satisfy a craving for happiness. Here we present a recipe for a great spring or summer salad that can be eaten as a meal or a side dish to any main course. The mixture of sweet and savory, and protein (eggs) and fats (avocado) will hold you through to your next meal, while making you feel light and happy as you endeavor your next activity.

INGREDIENTS

3   cups shredded spinach
3   cups arugula
2   cups cherry tomatoes
1   cucumber
2–3   cups of red grapes (seedless)
2   carrots
3   eggs
1   avocado
¼   cup of oil
4   tbsp. vinegar (or raspberry vinaigrette, if preferred)
Cottage cheese
Salt
Pepper

DIRECTIONS

Wash greens, fruits, and vegetables thoroughly in a strainer. On a cutting board, peel cucumbers (completely or partially, to preference), chop into cubes. Shred carrots or slice thinly, per preference. Peel and cube avocado.

In a small pot, place 3 eggs in some water (covering eggs) and bring to a boil. Boil for 10 minutes, drain, and place in cold water to chill. Set aside.

In a large mixing bowl, mix greens, cucumbers, and tomatoes. Place grapes along the perimeter of the bowl and a cluster in the middle. Place avocado along the inner perimeter, next to the grapes.

Remove eggs from water, peel outer shell, and cut in quarters. Place eggs in salad bowl, along the inner perimeter, next to the avocados. Next, arrange carrots next to the avocados.

Add a dollop of cottage cheese to the top of the salad.

Add salt and pepper to taste. Dress with oil and vinegar, or use raspberry vinaigrette dressing, if preferred.

Enjoyed best under the sun, with a cold glass of water.

Carrot Raisin Salad

Despite the inclusion of yogurt and honey, this salad is crunchier than most you will encounter, and because of the raisins and pineapple, has hidden moments of sweetness. And consider how simple is the road you must travel to find this bliss; a few ingredients, tossed together and chilled. The hardest part may be in having the patience to let it sit in the fridge. The weakest among us might dive right in.

INGREDIENTS

2 ¾	oz. plain Greek nonfat yogurt
½	oz. honey
5 ½	oz. canned pineapple tidbits
4	oz. fresh carrots
2	oz. raisins
1	oz. fresh celery

DIRECTIONS

Drain the pineapple tidbits and shred the carrots. Trim and dice the celery.

Combine the yogurt and the honey; whisk until they are well blended.

Add the remaining ingredients, tossing until everything is coated.

Cover, refrigerate and serve chilled.

Chicken Apple Walnut Salad

It's the salad that eats like a meal. There's nothing like sitting down with a chilled salad on a warm summer day. This one has diced chicken, fresh apple, red grapes, celery, and walnuts combined in a creamy yogurt dressing. Need we say more? This submitted recipe explores a wide variety of textures and even shapes, to say nothing of flavor combinations. Each bite can be different.

HONEY YOGURT DRESSING:

1 CUP YOGURT
2 TBSP. WARM HONEY
2 TBSP. APPLE CIDER VINEGAR
1 TBSP. LEMON JUICE
FRESHLY GROUND BLACK PEPPER AND SALT TO TASTE

SHAKE TOGETHER THE YOGURT, HONEY & VINEGAR IN A PINT JAR.

ADD THE LEMON JUICE AND SHAKE VIGOROUSLY.

ADD SALT AND PEPPER TO TASTE.

CHILL 1-2 HOURS BEFORE SERVING. SHAKE WELL BEFORE USE.

INGREDIENTS

¼   cup honey yogurt dressing
5¾   oz. diced cooked chicken
2¾   oz. fresh apples
1½   oz. seedless red grapes
¾   oz. fresh celery
¾   oz. walnut halves and pieces
1   tsp. fresh parsley
½   tsp. lemon juice
1   pinch black pepper

DIRECTIONS

Core and dice the apples into ½ inch cubes. Cut the grapes in half. Trim and dice the celery into ¼ inch pieces and mince the parsley.

Combine all the ingredients in a bowl and toss to mix. Chill before serving.

Collard Greens

Our submitting chef tells the story better than we ever could. "This recipe comes from my mother, who grew up in Georgia. She would cook this around Thanksgiving and Christmas, on special occasions, or when she thought of home. The smell brings me back to those times with my mother, and the time we took to slow-cook them together." Isn't this what cooking is all about?

INGREDIENTS

2–4 bunches of collard greens (no yellow around edges), removing the long stems

1 tbsp. salt

1 tsp. garlic powder

1 tsp. black pepper

1 smoked turkey leg or wing

2 small onions, finely chopped (a food processor is allowable for the fine texture)

2 small tomatoes for garnish (optional)

Red pepper (optional)

White vinegar (for cleaning collard greens)

DIRECTIONS

Clean collard greens thoroughly to remove grit. Roll 2-3 pieces like a cigar, chop up into a medium size. Add to a pot and let them soak in water, with white vinegar, for 30 minutes. Drain, rinse in a strainer, remove residue and grit from greens.

In a separate pot, add 4 to 6 cups of water, smoked turkey, salt, garlic powder, black pepper, and onions. Bring to a boil. Slowly add collard greens to the pot, stirring ingredients. Add more water, if necessary, as evaporation occurs. Cook for 2 to 3 hours, and taste for flavor and tenderness along the way. If the greens are still crunchy, then they are not ready yet.

After 2 hours, a lid can be added, but only half-way, to allow steam to escape. Finished product will have some water, but not much.

The juice can be saved for flavoring in other side dishes.

Optional garnishes: 2 small tomatoes, sliced thin, and added as a side garnish, along with some smoked turkey.

Servings: 2-4 meals. Store in refrigerator.

Potato Salad

Think picnics. Think summer days. Think green grass, light breezes, and sunshine. And think the center of Europe. While nobody can definitively trace the origins of this mixture of boiled potatoes and favored seasonings, we do know that it probably started somewhere in Germany centuries ago before spreading around the world. We also know that it continues to improve with every new version, every time a chef steps into a kitchen and says, "How can I make this recipe even better?" Try our submission and see what you think.

POTATOES:
TRY THIS RECIPE WITH WAXY, NEW, OR FINGERLING POTATOES, WHICH ARE LOWER IN STARCH. RED POTATOES WOULD BE A TASTY ADDITION AS WELL.

To save on fat and calories, use Miracle Whip Light or reduced-fat mayonnaise instead of regular Miracle Whip

Reduce the sodium in this recipe by using ½ tbsp. salt instead

INGREDIENTS

1   bag of potatoes
1½ cups of Miracle Whip™
1   cup sweet mixed pickles cut in quarters, or sweet relish
2   cups of egg whites
1   tbsp. Pink Himalayan salt
1   cup ice
2   tbsp. paprika

DIRECTIONS

Boil water in a pot and add Pink Himalayan salt. Boil on high for 4 to 8 minutes. Add whole potatoes. Loosely cover, leaving a vent, and boil for 10 to 15 minutes. Potatoes are done when they float and are easily poked with a fork.

Microwave egg whites in a microwave-safe bowl, covered for 3½ minutes. Cut into small cubes and place in the freezer.

Remove potatoes from heat and place into a strainer. Add ice while running cold water over the potatoes to quickly cool down the cooking process. Peel the potatoes under running water. Cut them into small cubes and place in a bowl.

Add Miracle Whip™, sweet pickles or relish, egg whites and stir until smooth. Sprinkle with paprika.

Refrigerate and enjoy.

Healthy Tips: The TLC Diet

THERAPEUTIC LIFESTYLE CHANGES: AN EATING PLAN TO LOWER CHOLESTEROL

CHOOSE LESS FOODS THAT HAVE SATURATED FAT OR TRANS FAT

- **Saturated fat:** found in fatty meat, poultry skin, processed meat, and full-fat dairy products
- **Trans fat:** found in margarine, shortening, fried foods, and packaged foods and baked goods (such as crackers, cookies, cakes, and pastries)

Eating less of these foods can help lower your LDL cholesterol.

CHOOSE MORE FOODS THAT HAVE HEART-HEALTHY FATS. GREAT SOURCES INCLUDE:

- **Fish:** best choices are salmon, tuna, mackerel, and sardines
- **Nuts:** best choices are walnuts or almonds. Limit yourself to one handful per day if watching your weight.
- **Flaxseed:** ground flaxseed can be sprinkled on many different foods, such as oatmeal or cereal, peanut butter toast, or added to smoothies. Aim to use 1 Tablespoon ground flaxseed each day.
- **Canola oil** and **soybean oil**

- **Avocado:** limit yourself to no more than ½ an avocado per day if watching your weight

Eating more of these foods can help lower your LDL cholesterol and raise your HDL cholesterol.

CHOOSE MORE FOODS WITH DIETARY FIBER. BEST SOURCES INCLUDE:

- **Fruits and vegetables:** especially when you eat the peel
- **Whole grains:** breads and crackers, as well as oatmeal, barley, and quinoa
- **Beans:** dry beans or canned beans. Canned beans should be rinsed before eating.
- **Flaxseed** (see above)

Eating more of these foods can help lower your LDL cholesterol and raise your HDL cholesterol.

- **Don't forget to exercise!** Exercising for 30 minutes each day can also help to lower LDL levels.meals will make it harder to manage your diabetes. Eat small, frequent meals and snacks to keep your blood sugar and energy levels in check.

WHAT IS CHOLESTEROL?

Cholesterol is a substance in our blood. Our bodies need a small amount of cholesterol in order to function properly. There are two different kinds of cholesterol: the "good" kind is called HDL (or high density lipoprotein), and the "bad" kind is called LDL (or low density lipoprotein). When our levels of HDL get too low and our levels of LDL get too high, it makes it harder for our heart to work properly.

WHAT ARE THERAPEUTIC LIFESTYLE CHANGES (TLC)?

TLC is an eating plan for people with high cholesterol that focuses on foods that will help to lower LDL levels and raise HDL levels in the blood. The food we eat can often affect our cholesterol levels, so changing our diet can help to change our cholesterol levels and bring them closer to a healthy range.

CHOLESTEROL GOALS	
TOTAL CHOLESTEROL	< 200 mg/dL
HDL	> 60 mg/dL
LDL	< 100 mg/dL

TLC DIET BASICS

	FOODS TO CHOOSE MORE OF	FOODS TO CHOOSE LESS OF
MEATS AND PROTEIN FOODS	Poultry without skin, fish, beans and peas, seeds, nuts, and nut butter	Poultry with skin Beef (hamburger, steak) Bacon, sausage, Fried meats
FATS AND OILS	Olive, peanut, soy and canola oil Vegetable oil spreads (such as Smart Balance™)	Butter, stick margarine Shortening
GRAINS	Whole grain breads and cereals Whole wheat pasta Brown rice Oats, barley, quinoa	Baked goods (doughnuts, biscuits, croissants, pastries, pies, cookies) Fried, packaged snack foods (chips, cheese pus, crackers)
VEGETABLES	Fresh, frozen, canned or vegetables without added fat	Fried vegetables
FRUIT	Fresh, frozen, canned or dried fruit	Fried fruits
MILK AND DAIRY	Skim or 1% milk Nonfat or low-fat yogurt or cottage cheese Fat-free or low-fat cheese	Whole or 2% milk Cream, half & half Full-fat cheese Cream cheese, sour cream

TLC SAMPLE MEAL PLANS

	DAY 1	DAY 2
BREAKFAST	¾ cup oatmeal with skim milk 1 banana Coffee with skim milk	1 apple Whole grain cereal (Wheaties™, Cheerios™, Raisin Bran™, etc.) with skim milk Coffee with skim milk
MORNING SNACK	Whole grain crackers with peanut butter	Celery sticks with hummus
LUNCH	1 cup homemade vegetable and barley soup 2 slices whole grain bread with vegetable oil spread Diced mango or papaya Water with lemon or lime	Garden salad (lettuce, tomato, cucumber, carrots) with tuna Low-fat Italian dressing 1 slice whole grain bread with vegetable oil spread Water with lemon or lime
AFTERNOON SNACK	¼ cup unsalted almonds ¼ cup dried fruit	¾ cup low-fat yogurt ½ cup fresh berries
DINNER	Broiled salmon with lemon Collard greens sauteed in canola oil Roasted yams Brown rice 1 cup skim milk	Beans and rice dish Roasted carrots Cauliflower and broccoli meledy Small whole grain dinner roll Water with lemon or lime

HIV: Modes of transmission and modes of prevention

Modes of Transmission

As discussed in the previous chapter, there are specific ways that HIV can be transmitted, including:

→ **1) Sexual activity**
→ **2) Sharing needles**
→ **3) Mother-child transmission (vertical transmission)**

Let's take a closer look at exactly what this means:

SEXUAL ACTIVITY

HIV CAN BE TRANSMITTED SEXUALLY VIA THE FOLLOWING BODILY FLUIDS:

- SEMEN
- PRE-SEMINAL FLUIDS
- VAGINAL FLUIDS
- RECTAL FLUIDS
- BLOOD

SHARING NEEDLES

HIV CAN BE TRANSMITTED VIA NEEDLES IN THE FOLLOWING CIRCUMSTANCES:

- SHARING NEEDLES FOR MEDICINAL OR RECREATIONAL DRUG USAGE
- BLOOD TRANSFUSIONS (BLOOD IS SCREENED TODAY PRIOR TO PATIENT TRANSFUSION)

MOTHER-TO-CHILD

HIV CAN BE VERTICALLY TRANSMITTED TO A CHILD IN THE FOLLOWING WAYS:

- DURING UTERINE DEVELOPMENT
- DURING BIRTH
- THROUGH BREASTFEEDING

THE FOLLOWING ARE *NOT* WAYS THAT HIV CAN BE TRANSMITTED:

- SALIVA
- TEARS
- KISSING (CLOSED MOUTH)
- HUGGING
- HOLDING HANDS
- INSECTS
- PETS
- SHARING FOOD OR DRINKS
- SHARING PENS, PENCILS, DOORKNOBS, TOILETS, ETC.
- AIR
- WATER

REFERENCE

The Basics of HIV Prevention. (2021). The Basics of HIV Prevention. [ONLINE] Available at: https://hivinfo.nih.gov/ understanding-hiv/fact-sheets/ basics-hiv-prevention. [Accessed 24 March 2021].

Modes of Prevention

Let's learn how to prevent HIV by following these risk-reduction guidelines:

1 GET TESTED FOR HIV (AND ALL STIS)

- TAKE CONTROL OF YOUR STATUS AND GET TESTED PRIOR TO SEX AND AT LEAST EVERY 3-6 MONTHS IF YOU ARE SEXUALLY ACTIVE AND HAVE MULTIPLE PARTNERS. BEST PRACTICE IS TO HAVE AN HIV TEST EVERY 6-12 MONTHS.
- TALK TO YOUR PARTNERS AND MAKE TESTING AN ACTIVITY YOU DO TOGETHER.

2 WEAR CONDOMS EVERY TIME YOU HAVE SEX

- CONDOMS ARE AVAILABLE FOR FREE AT ALL HEALTH CENTERS, AND MOST COMMUNITY BASED ORGANIZATIONS.

3 TRY LESS RISKY SEXUAL ACTIVITIES, SUCH AS ORAL SEX

- HIV IS MAINLY SPREAD THROUGH UNPROTECTED VAGINAL AND/OR ANAL SEX.

4 DO NOT INJECT DRUGS

- IF YOU DO, USE NEW AND STERILE DRUG INJECTION EQUIPMENT EACH TIME AND NEVER SHARE WITH ANYONE ELSE.

5 REDUCE NUMBER OF SEXUAL PARTNERS

- HAVING MULTIPLE PARTNERS INCREASES THE RISK OF HIV OR STI INFECTION.
- IF YOU HAVE MULTIPLE PARTNERS, COMMUNICATE TO THEM ABOUT THE IMPORTANCE OF GETTING REGULARLY TESTED FOR HIV AND STIS AND REGULAR USE OF CONDOMS DURING SEX.

6 CONSIDER PRE-EXPOSURE PROPHYLAXIS (PrEP)

- PrEP IS A ONCE-A-DAY MEDICATION THAT PREVENTS PERSONS AT-RISK FOR HIV FROM CONTRACTING THE VIRUS.
- IN MASSACHUSETTS, THE COST OF MEDICATION AND CO-PAYS ARE FREE FOR MOST PEOPLE.
- TALK TO YOUR HEALTHCARE PROVIDER TO SEE IF PREP IS RIGHT FOR YOU.

3
Entrees

WHAT'S YOUR PLEASURE?
CHICKEN, PORK, BEEF, FISH,
RICE, BEANS, POTATO? YOU'RE
GUARANTEED TO FIND SOMETHING
TO SATISFY YOUR CRAVINGS.

Caribbean Chicken Pelau

Pelau is a dish native to the French West Indies that can be prepared with either beef or chicken. Our submitted recipe calls for the latter, the more traditional choice. Skin the chicken but use the full pieces.

We recommend using ½-1tsp salt to make this recipe more heart healthy

Substitute olive or canola oil in place of butter to lower the saturated fat

Reduce to ½ cup for less added sugar

Try reduced-fat coconut milk (it tastes very similar) to lower the saturated fat in this recipe

We recommend adding them in. The more vegetables in your diet the better.

INGREDIENTS

CARIBBEAN GREEN SEASONING

3	tbsp. chives
2	tbsp. thyme
1	tbsp. oregano
1	tbsp. parsley
1	tbsp. shado beni or cilantro leaves
4	cloves of garlic

CHICKEN PELAU

1	lb. chicken wings
1	lb. chicken legs
1	lb. chicken neck
1	lb. chicken back
2	tsp. Caribbean green seasoning
1½	tsp. salt
1	cup green pigeon peas
1	tbsp. butter
¾	cup sugar, white or brown
1	cup water
1	cup coconut milk
2	cups of brown rice
2	carrots, chopped
1	small onion, chopped
1	clove garlic, finely chopped
5	spring onions (scallions)
	(Green, red and yellow peppers optional)

DIRECTIONS

CARIBBEAN GREEN SEASONING

Green seasoning is prepared by combining 3 tbsp. chives, 2 tbsp. thyme, 1 tbsp. oregano, 1tbsp. parsley, 1 tbsp. shado beni or cilantro leaves, and 4 cloves of garlic in a food processor. Alternatively, use a blender with 2 tbsp. vinegar. Final result will be a thick paste.

CHICKEN PELAU

If using dried peas, soak them in water overnight in three cups of water; drain; boil 3 cups of water and add the peas; simmer for 15 minutes, or until cooked almost all the way through; drain and set aside. If using canned peas, drain, rinse them with cold water and set aside.

Marinate chicken with Caribbean green seasoning and 1½ teaspoons of salt for at least 20-30 minutes, if not overnight.

In a medium pot on high heat add 1 tbsp butter and ¾ cup of sugar, caramelizing until golden brown. Add marinated chicken with the rest of the marinade, using a spatula to coat the chicken well. Add water and coconut milk. Bring to a boil and set to medium heat so that the chicken and peas are cooked until the chicken starts to fall off the bones. Season with salt as desired.

Wash rice and add after 20 to 30 minutes, with carrots, onion, garlic, spring onions and peppers. Bring back to a boil. Reduce heat to simmer until rice is cooked through to your liking (Hint: In the Caribbean, we especially like it to be a bit moist!).

Brie & Spinach Stuffed Chicken Breast

Stuffing meats with tender surprises is a tradition that goes back at least to the Roman Empire, as at least one ancient cookbook, *Apicius De Re Coquinaria,* holds several such recipes, including for stuffing chicken. Through the ages, we've experimented with many combinations, and our entry is one of the most delectable around, offering multiple layers of flavor and a couple of textures as well.

INGREDIENTS

Using more spinach will add extra nutrition to this recipe!

Consider reducing to 1 tsp. of salt

2-4	chicken breasts
4-8	brie wedge slices
2-4	cups spinach, coarsely chopped
1	tsp. parsley
½	tsp. celery seed
1	tsp. thyme
1	tsp. rosemary, crushed
2	tsp. olive oil
2	tsp. Pink Himalayan salt, separated
2	tsp. pepper, separated
16 -32	toothpicks

DIRECTIONS

Preheat the oven to 350.

Halve breasts on flat side, leaving ½ inch connected, enough to fold over inner ingredients. Cover and set aside in the fridge.

Slice brie into thin, long slices to fit inside the chicken breasts.

In a bowl, combine spinach, parsley, celery seed, thyme, rosemary, olive oil, 1 tsp. of Pink Himalayan salt, and 1 tsp. pepper, and mix thoroughly. Spread mixture on inner bottom half of chicken breasts.

Top with brie slices, close, and pin each breast shut with 8 toothpicks.

Arrange in a nonstick square or rectangle pan. Season with remaining Pink Himalayan salt and pepper. Cook covered for 35 minutes, then uncovered to brown for 10 minutes.

Chicken Teriyaki

The Japanese consider teriyaki to be a cooking technique, and, well, they invented it, so they get to do whatever they want with it. In the United States, we've appended the name to any dish in which we use teriyaki sauce, like this one and our entry for Pork & Vegetable Teriyaki (see page 46). Broken down, the word refers to the shine from the sugar content *(teri)* and the grilling method *(yaki).* But if you ask any American what teriyaki means, they'll respond with one word: "Yum."

INGREDIENTS

Choose low-sodium store-bought teriyaki sauce if you can!

TERIYAKI SAUCE

3	tbsp. teriyaki sauce
3	tbsp. water
2	pinches minced garlic
1	pinch ginger
2	tbsp. + ¾ tsp. orange juice
2.88	grams cornstarch

CHICKEN

1	tbsp. + 1 tsp. vegetable oil
12	oz. chicken thighs, diced
4	oz. broccoli florets
3	oz. cabbage
2	oz. carrots
2	oz. celery
2	oz. yellow onion

DIRECTIONS

TERIYAKI SAUCE

To make the teriyaki sauce, combine sauce, water, garlic, and ginger in a pot over medium-high heat. Bring to a boil.

Mix orange juice and cornstarch in a cup to form a slurry. Add the slurry to the pot, whisking constantly, until mixture thickens and boils.

Reduce heat and let simmer for two minutes.

CHICKEN

For the main dish, heat 1 tbsp. of oil in a wok over high heat. Add chicken. Stir-fry until browned, about 4 to 6 minutes.

Remove the chicken from the pan, and then add the broccoli. Stir-fry the broccoli for two minutes and then add the cabbage, carrot, celery, and onion. Stir-fry until the vegetables are tender-crisp, about 2 to 3 minutes.

Add cooked chicken and 1 cup of teriyaki sauce. Stir-fry until everything is coated and heated through.

Fried Fish

Travel the world over and you will find many variations on the simple theme of fried fish. It's a symbol of the days of the British Empire, a classic French dish, and a staple of American cuisine. But to truly experience seafood at its best, visit the island nations of the Caribbean. If you can't get there right now, try our submitted recipe.

White fish is a healthy and lean form of protein. Frying fish can add extra fat and calories. While this recipe is a lighter pan-fried version of fried fish, you can make it even lighter by oven-frying.

To oven fry: Line a baking sheet with foil and spray generously with cooking spray. Add the prepared fish and spray the fish with cooking spray. Cook for about 10 minutes on each side in a 400 degree oven. This gives you crispy fish without the extra fat.

INGREDIENTS

2–4 filets of white fish
(haddock, cod, tilapia, or preferred mild white fish)

½ cup of oil (canola, vegetable, or peanut)

Lemon or orange juice, freshly squeezed

Salt

Pepper

Flour

DIRECTIONS

Rinse the fish, pat dry with a paper towel, and place on a plate. Squeeze either fresh lemon or orange on the fish, rubbing it all over to penetrate the meat. Add salt and pepper to desired flavor. Let the fish sit for one hour.

In a skillet, place ½ cup of oil on medium heat. To test if oil is hot enough, place a drop of water on the skillet, and if it sizzles, then the oil is ready.

Take fish and dip both sides in flour on a plate, coating lightly. Carefully place the filets into the oil on the skillet.

Cook on medium heat for two to three minutes per side, flipping to ensure both sides are golden brown.

Remove from heat, place on a plate, and add more lemon or orange if desired.

Serving suggestion: Serve over rice and beans.

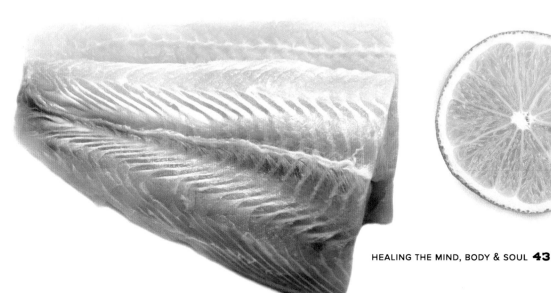

Cotelette de porc sur puree de patates a la sauce aux beteraves

Translated from the original and beautiful French, that's "pork chop on mashed sweet potatoes with beet sauce." In any language, it sounds delightful. And, a tip from the chef who submitted this recipe is that it doesn't need to be pork. Veal, or any other meat or fish, can be substituted to suit your needs.

INGREDIENTS

Save on saturated fat by reducing to ½–¾ stick of butter

Try substituting whole or 2% milk to reduce saturated fat

1–2 cut pork chops
1 sweet potato
3 young beets (red)
1 stick of butter
½ cup olive oil
½ cup parmesan cheese
1 tbsp. lemon juice
1 tsp. lemon zest
½ cup evaporated milk or cream
1–2 tbsp. vinegar
Salt, pepper, coarse cane sugar

DIRECTIONS

Marinate meat with chosen spices in lemon juice and vinegar. Put in refrigerator for six hours or overnight.

Boil beets and potato in a separate pot in lightly salted water for 15-20 minutes, until cooked but firm. Peel the sweet potato and cut and put aside 2-3 rectangular pieces for later. Mash the remaining with 1 tbsp. of butter, ¼ cup of milk, and parmesan cheese to your taste to obtain a smooth puree. Peel two beets for garnish and blend the other one in a blender with lemon juice and vinegar. Sift through a strainer to obtain a juice that you will reduce in a pan. Add 1 tbsp. of butter and sugar to obtain a nice red sauce. Add salt and pepper to taste.

Brown both sides of the pork in butter and olive oil in a skillet. Transfer to the oven and bake at 375 degrees for 20 to 30 minutes until cooked to desired tenderness.

Serve pork chop over the puree on a nice oval plate with the sliced beets in two halves on top of the three rectangular pieces of potatoes. Use 1-2 tsbp. of the red sauce over the pork.

PHOTOS: STOCK.ADOBE.COM/ VOLFF

Cranberry–Glazed Pork Roast

Southeastern Massachusetts is cranberry country, and that's not just a slogan. Cranberry farming began on Cape Cod in the 1800s. And yet, we still consider cranberry to be generally a Thanksgiving-specific fruit. One taste of this cranberry-glazed pork roast, and you will be convinced that cranberries can be used any time of year. We will admit, though, that it feels like this dish would go well on a cool fall evening, or even a cold winter's night.

INGREDIENTS

1	lb. 2 oz. center-cut boneless pork loin
¼	tsp. kosher salt
2	pinches black pepper

FOR GLAZE

8	oz. canned cranberry sauce
2	cups orange juice
2	cups sherry
2	tbsp. ground nutmeg
2	tbsp. ground cinnamon
2	tbsp. fresh orange zest
2	tsp. kosher salt

DIRECTIONS

CRANBERRY GLAZE

To prepare glaze, bring cranberry sauce, orange juice, sherry, nutmeg, cinnamon, orange zest and 2 tsp. kosher salt to a boil in a pot over medium-high heat. Reduce heat, simmer, stirring constantly, until thickened, for about 4 to 5 minutes. Let cool.

PORK ROAST

Preheat oven to 325 F. Season pork with salt and pepper to taste. Place pork fat-side up on a rack in a roasting pan. Roast until internal temperature reaches 125 F, about 45 to 75 minutes.

Pour ⅓ cup cranberry glaze over pork. Roast until internal temperature reaches 145 F, about 15 minutes. Let rest about 30 minutes before slicing.

Pork and Vegetable Teriyaki

We've Americanized teriyaki. We've blended it into hamburger meat and eaten it in buns, for goodness' sake. This, though, is a sign of the world coming together, adapting great cuisine for their own needs, desires, circumstances, and even quirks. The Japanese mainly use teriyaki with fish, but there are many other ways to enjoy the benefits of a good teriyaki sauce. Swap out the meat, play with vegetable combinations, and you have a completely new dish.

INGREDIENTS

TERIYAKI SAUCE

3	tbsp. teriyaki sauce
3	tbsp. water
2	pinches minced garlic
1	pinch ginger
2	tbsp. + ¾ tsp. orange juice
2.88	grams cornstarch

Choose low-sodium teriyaki sauce if you can

PORK AND VEGETABLES

1	tbsp. + 1 tsp. vegetable oil
1	lb. center cut pork loin, cut into pieces
1	tsp. gingerroot, minced
1	tsp. garlic, minced
4½	oz. carrots
4	oz. yellow onion
3	oz. cabbage
2	oz. red peppers
2	oz. celery
½	oz. green onions

DIRECTIONS

TERIYAKI SAUCE

To make the teriyaki sauce, combine sauce, water, garlic, and ginger in a pot over medium-high heat. Bring to a boil.

Mix orange juice and cornstarch in a cup to form a slurry. Add the slurry to the pot, whisking constantly, until mixture thickens and boils. Reduce heat and let simmer for two minutes.

PORK AND VEGETABLES

For the main dish, slice carrots lengthwise, and then diagonally. Cut the yellow onion and the cabbage into 1-inch pieces. Remove the seeds from the red peppers and cut into 1-inch squares. Trim the celery and slice diagonally into ¼-inch pieces. Trim the green onions and slice into ⅛-inch pieces.

Heat 1 tbsp. of oil in a wok over high heat. Add the pork and stir-fry until browned, about 2 to 3 minutes. Remove the pork from the pan, and then add the gingerroot, garlic, yellow onion, cabbage, pepper, and celery. Stir-fry it all until the vegetables are tender-crisp, about 2 to 3 minutes. Add cooked pork and 4 oz. of teriyaki sauce. Stir-fry until everything is coated and heated through, about 30 seconds. Add green onions after plating the rest of the dish.

Strawberry Beef

Does it sound too good to be true? The idea of pairing fruits with meats doesn't come naturally to us, as we generally look to vegetables when we consider building a menu alongside a good piece of steak. And yet, with a little adventurousness, we can walk a little bit on the wild side, playing with spice combinations to bring out the best in both worlds. Take this dish on its own or place it over some white rice. So, to answer our opening question? Oh, it's true.

INGREDIENTS

1	tbsp. olive oil
8 – 12	strawberries, quartered, set aside in fridge
½ – 1	lbs. steak tips cut into cubes
1	tbsp. parsley
1	tbsp. basil
½	tbsp. sage
1	tbsp. oregano
½	tsp. Pink Himalayan salt
1	tsp. pepper
1	tbsp. garlic, freshly chopped

Remove any large chunks of visible fat (the solid white part of the meat) before cooking

DIRECTIONS

Add olive oil to a pan on medium heat, then add chopped garlic. Sauté garlic for 2 minutes.

Slowly add steak tips to the pan. Once all steak tips are in the pan, stir occasionally until the meat has started to brown.

Add parsley, basil, sage, oregano, pepper, and Pink Himalayan salt. Continue cooking for 5 to 10 more minutes until the meat is about done.

Lower the heat to low. Add strawberries and fold into the steak tips, let simmer for 1 minute. Turn off heat.

Enjoy on top of your favorite side.

Beef Stroganoff

The description is simple: tender beef cubes, mushrooms and onions in a savory sour cream sauce. Beef Stroganoff first hit Russian cookbooks in the 1870s and has undergone numerous tweaks through time. Some are minor, including which side dishes go best with it, and how to cut the beef (do you prefer cubes or strips?), while others substitute other meats for the beef. Generally, Americans prefer it served over rice or noodles.

INGREDIENTS

Choose low-fat or fat-free sour cream or plain yogurt for a lower-fat recipe

Try low-sodium beef base

1½	oz. sour cream
1	tbsp. dijon mustard
2	tsp. vegetable oil
1	lb. round eye beef, cubed
1½	oz. diced yellow onion
4¾	oz. fresh mushrooms
¼	oz. beef base
¾	oz. flour
2	cups water
¼	tsp. kosher salt
⅛	tsp. black pepper
2	tsp. parsley, minced

DIRECTIONS

Combine sour cream, and dijon mustard. Whisk until well blended.

Heat oil in a pot over medium-high heat. Add beef in batches, sautéing until well-browned on all sides. Remove the beef from the pot and set aside.

Add onions and mushrooms to the drippings in the pot. Sauté the onion until it is translucent, about 3 to 5 minutes. Stir in the beef base. Add flour and whisk until blended. Cook for about 4 minutes, whisking often.

Add water, salt, and pepper. Whisk until well blended. Cook, whisking constantly, until the mixture thickens and boils. Add the browned beef. Return to a boil and then reduce heat. Cover and let simmer for about 45 to 55 minutes, until beef is tender.

Add the sour cream mixture. Cook, stirring constantly, until the mixture is heated through. Do not boil. Stir in parsley. Serve hot.

Hearty Meat Sauce

It's not even a full meal, but when we put forth recipes for it, we treat it like it is. Some Italian homes just aren't really considered homes unless there is a good sauce simmering on the stove for most of the day. Add some meat to it and it gains heartiness.

INGREDIENTS

Choose 90% lean or higher ground beef or try ground turkey instead

4	oz. ground beef
¾	oz. yellow onion
¼	oz. red pepper
¼	oz. green pepper
2.66	grams garlic, minced
½	cup + 1 tbsp. diced tomatoes
½	oz. tomato paste
¼	tsp. red wine vinegar
⅛	tsp. dried basil
⅛	tsp. oregano
1	pinch black pepper

DIRECTIONS

Sauté beef in a pot on medium-high heat until no longer pink, 8 to 10 minutes. Drain off fat.

Add onion, peppers and garlic. Sauté until onion is tender-crisp, 2 to 3 minutes. Add remaining ingredients. Mix well.

Bring to a boil. Reduce heat. Simmer until sauce has thickened, for about 20 to 30 minutes. Cover.

Serve over your favorite pasta.

Meatloaf

This is a go-to recipe for a Sunday dinner, or a weeknight when you want something homecooked without too much fuss. Pairs well with sweet potatoes (mashed with butter), salad, sweat peas, or corn. And there is just something to the term "comfort food" and the way that it pairs with meatloaf. The intrinsic warmth coming from the inside of the dish that transfers right into the belly then spreads to the soul.
Let's face it; life goes well with meatloaf.

INGREDIENTS

1	lb. of ground beef or turkey (90% lean)
1	green bell pepper
1	medium onion
2	eggs, beaten
1	can of breadcrumbs (regular or Italian style)
1	cup water (to add hydration to the mixture)

Saison (or all-purpose seasoning)

Optional: beef or turkey gravy, or a can of tomato paste

1 loaf pan (large) or 2-3 small loaf pans for individualized servings

Cooking spray (to grease loaf pans)

DIRECTIONS

Wash pepper. Peel and wash onion. On a cutting board, finely chop onion and pepper (either by hand or in a food processor). Separate into two separate bowls and set aside.

Coat inside of a loaf pan with cooking spray and preheat the oven to 350 degrees.

In a large bowl, mix ground meat and 2 beaten eggs, along with preferred seasoning. Wash your hands and add breadcrumbs and water to bowl as you go, mixing with hands, and ensuring that a spongey texture is attained. (Do not add too much water at first; more can be added later to make the meat more moist, if it is not spongey enough.) Add onions to meat mixture, and mix in. Do the same with the peppers.

Add meat mixture to loaf pan, and fill about ¾ full. Place in oven, uncovered, for 35 minutes. Take out, check color (it should be slightly browned on top), and stick a fork in to see if the meatloaf is cooking through.

If you're interested in a moister meatloaf, add gravy or tomato paste, applying with a spatula, spreading evenly on the top of the meatloaf.

Cover pan and place back in the oven for an additional 10-15 minutes.

Country Meatloaf

In 2007, *Good Housekeeping* magazine took a poll asking Americans to rate their favorite dishes. Meatloaf came in at number seven. Not bad, but also not surprising. Meatloaf had its rise in the United States during the Great Depression, when Americans cobbled together whatever they could find, including crackers and breadcrumbs, to create nourishing and sustaining dishes to feed their families. From those dark days a great American tradition was born. Our submitted recipe captures that good, old country feel, with a few twists of its own.

You could use ground turkey for all of the meat in this recipe to make it lower in fat, saturated fat and calories. If you'd like to keep the beef flavor, consider doing ½ turkey and ½ beef.

INGREDIENTS

1¼	oz. diced yellow onion
2	pinches beef base
1	tbsp. plus 1 tsp. water
1	tsp. Montreal steak seasoning
7	oz. ground beef
4¾	oz. ground turkey
1½	oz. eggs
1	oz. breadcrumbs
½	tsp. dry mustard
⅛	tsp. dried thyme

DIRECTIONS

Preheat oven to 300 F. In a pan coated with cooking spray over medium-high heat, sauté onion until lightly caramelized, about 5 to 6 minutes. Stir in base. Add water and seasoning. Bring to a boil. Cook until liquid is evaporated, 4 to 5 minutes. Let cool.

In a mixing bowl, combine beef, turkey, eggs, breadcrumbs, mustard, thyme, and onion mixture. Mix on low speed until well combined, 4 to 5 minutes.

Shape meat mixture into a loaf, about 4 inches by 16 inches. Place on parchment-lined half sheet pans. Bake until internal temperature reaches 165 F, about 30 to 35 minutes. Let rest 10 minutes. Drain. Cut into 12 slices.

Sweet Potato Casserole

This recipe was passed down from a grandmother to a mother, to our current chef. It was traditionally made for family gatherings on holidays like July 4th, Thanksgiving, and Christmas, and especially for summer cookouts. And so it has gone with Americans and their love of the sweet potato. In three states — Alabama, Louisiana, and North Carolina — it's the state vegetable. Starting out as a favored dish in the south, candied sweet potatoes can now be found on tables across the country.

Reducing the sugar, marshmallows and butter in this dish, will make it not as sweet, but still tasty and a little better for you. We recommend cutting each measurement in half for a slightly healthier version.

Try 1 pound of brown sugar instead of 2

Use ½ the bag of marshmallows

Reduce to ½ a stick of butter

INGREDIENTS

4–5 large sweet potatoes
2 lbs. light brown sugar
1 bag of small marshmallows
1 stick of butter, room temperature
Cooking spray (to grease dish)

DIRECTIONS

Pre-heat oven to 275 degrees.

Wash sweet potatoes in cool water and peel the skin off. On a cutting board, cube potatoes and place back into water. Rinse.

Fill a large pot with cold water, place on stove and bring to boil. Cook potatoes until tender (test them by inserting a fork; when there is no resistance, they're ready). Drain, and place back in pot.

In a large mixing bowl, combine butter and a few tablespoons of brown sugar, along with potatoes. Use a spatula to rotate the potatoes to coat in the butter and sugar. Do not mash the potatoes.

Spray a casserole dish with cooking spray, coat with some brown sugar and add marshmallows to cover the bottom of the dish. Add a layer of sweet potatoes, and repeat the layers of sugar with marshmallows, followed by potatoes, until the dish is ¾ full. The top layer should be more butter, sugar, and marshmallows. Cover with tin foil and place in oven for 15 minutes. Uncover, and place back in oven for an additional 30-45 minutes, checking for caramelization of sugar. Remove from oven.

Purees de Pommes de Terre aux Andouilles ou a la Viande Moulue

This recipe is a bit more involved than many you will find in this cookbook, but you'll find the result worth the wait. Potatoes, or *pommes de terre,* are a staple of Haitian cuisine and this mashed recipe calls for you to make a choice: ground beef, turkey, pork or andouille sausage?

Use leaner ground meat to lower the total fat in this recipe. Look for 90% lean or higher. Ground turkey is also a leaner substitute.

Using milk instead of cream will make this recipe lower in fat and calories.

INGREDIENTS

1	lb. ground meat or ground andouilles
½	cup chopped onion
¼	cup chopped shallots
3	tbsp. red wine vinegar
2-3	tbsp. garlic powder
3	tbsp. lemon juice
¼	cup breadcrumbs
1	tbsp. mustard
1	hot pepper
1	egg
½	cup chopped red and green pepper
3-4	tbsp. tomato paste
¼	cup of water
4	potatoes
½	cup parmesan cheese
¼	cup cream or milk
1	tbsp. melted butter
Salt	
Ground pepper	

DIRECTIONS

Mix ground meat with chopped onion, shallots, vinegar, 2 tbsp. garlic powder, 2 tbsp. lemon juice, breadcrumbs, and mustard, with salt, dark ground pepper, and hot pepper to taste. Let stand for 15 to 20 minutes.

Heat a quarter-cup of olive oil in a pot, add prepared ground meat, toss until brown. Add tomato paste and some water. Mix well to eliminate clumps. Let cook for 15 minutes.

In a separate pot, place whole potatoes in salted water and bring them to a boil until potatoes are well-cooked.

In a bowl, remove the potato skins and then mash the cooked potatoes. Add parmesan cheese, cream, butter, 1 tbsp. of garlic powder, salt, and black or white pepper.

Preheat the oven to 300 degrees. Grease the bottom of a baking pan with either oil or 1 tbsp. of melted butter.

Add mashed potato first, then a layer of cooked meat, etc., alternating. The top layer should be of mashed potato.

Sprinkle the top with parmesan cheese. Bake until top is crispy brown. Approximately 15-20 minutes.

Riz aux Poix Rouges

Haitians consider this rice and beans delight, also called *diri kolé ak pwa,* their national dish. It can be made with a variety of beans, and our submission calls for one of the favorites: kidney beans. The recipe has deep ties to the era of slavery in Haiti, which ended with the declaration of Haitian independence on January 1, 1804. While they were definitely done with slavery, Haitians were not quick to give up this simple yet flavorful combination.

Try substituting with a lower-fat turkey- or chicken-based sausage.

Use brown rice for more fiber.

Use reduced-sodium broth to make this recipe a bit more heart healthy.

INGREDIENTS

1   cup of dry kidney beans
3   cups of water
3   tbsp. of olive oil
½   cup of anduis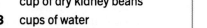
     (sliced Andouille sausage; more or less as desired)
¼   cup of tritris
     (Haitian dried shrimp)
2   cloves of garlic
2   cups rice
1   cup chicken broth
Salt, pepper
Bouquet garni (thyme, persil [parsley], 2-3 cloves heads, 1 laurel leaf)

DIRECTIONS

Prepare the beans by soaking them for 12 hours in water.

Drain the beans and boil them with the bouquet garni in two cups of water for 40 minutes or until al-dente. (The herbs can be tied into a small "bouquet," or placed in a cheesecloth bag, to help flavor the mixture).

Drain the water from the beans, keeping 1 cup for later.

In a pot, add olive oil, beans, anduis, tritri, salt, and pepper until fried. Put aside.

Add the water set aside from boiling the beans and the chicken broth together in a pot. Bring to boil until reduced to about 1½ cups.

Add the rice and cook uncovered until the water is almost gone.

Add the fried beans mixture, stirring it into the rice. Cover the pot for 15 to 30 minutes until rice is well-cooked.

Add salt to taste as desired.

Rice and Beans

There is nothing so unifying as familiar food. Traverse the globe and you will find innumerable representations of the simple combination of two staple foods, rice and beans. It becomes an instant conversation starter wherever we go. What beans do you use? What's that spice I'm tasting? How long do you cook it for? It's a dish that proves that despite distances, we have universally shared commonalities.

Using less oil in the rice will lower the overall fat and calories in this recipe

INGREDIENTS

1   lb. bag of black or red kidney beans, dried
1   onion, chopped
1   tbsp. garlic powder
2–3 tbsp. olive or peanut oil for beans, 2-4 tbsp. for rice
4   cups of white rice — jasmine or enriched long grain
2–4 cups of water for beans, 10 cups for rice
Salt
Pepper
Parsley for garnish (optional)

DIRECTIONS

Wash beans thoroughly in a strainer to remove grit. Place them in a pot (a Dutch oven is ideal), cover, and bring to a boil for 2 minutes. Remove from heat and let sit covered for 1 to 4 hours. The longer they are left sitting, the more tender the beans will be for re-cooking.

Drain the beans. Place the beans back in the pot with 2-4 cups of water (enough to cover the beans), chopped onion, and garlic powder (add more to suit your taste if desired). Boil for 1 hour, or until the beans become tender (do not overcook beans, or they will dissolve). Strain any excess water. The mixture should not be soupy. Add salt and pepper to taste. Add 2-3 tablespoons of peanut or olive oil.

Wash rice in a strainer. Place in a pot (a Dutch oven is preferred). Add water (up to 10 cups), salt, pepper, 2-4 tablespoons of oil, and place on medium heat. Bring to a boil. Reduce heat, simmer, cover, and cook rice until it is tender, and the liquid is absorbed, about 15-20 minutes. Remove from heat and fluff with fork.

To serve, place some rice in a bowl, add some beans on top of rice. Add a teaspoon of oil, salt and pepper if desired, and garnish with parsley.

Egg Yolk Marinated in Soy Sauce on Rice

All three ingredients are in the title! Koreans know this recipe as *shoyu zuke ranou*. Our champion for this recipe suggests that you wash your rice well, rinsing it at least twice or until the water runs clear after swishing the rice through. Unwashed rice holds starch that makes it clumpy and sticky. This recipe includes marinating the yolks, so be prepared to eat this delicacy one, two or three days in the future. Multiply out the number of yolks and amount of soy sauce needed to fit your desire.

INGREDIENTS

1 egg yolk
2 tbsp. soy sauce
White rice

Use reduced-sodium soy sauce as more heart healthy alternative.

Try brown rice for more fiber!

DIRECTIONS

Separate egg yolks from egg whites and place the yolks in a small container.

Drizzle the soy sauce slowly into the container and on top of the yolks, so as not to break the yolks. They do not need to be submerged in soy sauce but be sure there is enough to let the yolks marinate.

Depending on how long you marinate the yolks, it produces different effects. The yolk hardens up just by being marinated.

1 day = Slightly hard on the outside, poke it and the inside will still be gooey.
2 days = The outside hardens, inside is sticky and less gooey.
3 days = The yolk is sticky and firm.

Prepare white rice in a quantity fitting the number of yolks you have chosen to prepare.

Place the chilled egg yolks over your warm rice and drizzle some of the marinated soy sauce over the rice or save it for a soup.

Moi Moi

To find the best Moi Moi, a steamed bean pudding, one must travel to Western Nigeria. Luckily, we have local expertise. Moi Moi can be quite versatile. Our recipe submitter says to consider adding hard-boiled eggs, cut into small pieces, or corned beef, either blended into the mixture or on the side. Tomato puree gives Moi Moi its classic color. Nutmeg gives it its taste. Avoid using hot water, as it can cause lumps. And avoid fragrant oils, as they can alter the flavor.

INGREDIENTS

Look for lower-sodium bouillon to reduce the salt content

Try reducing the amount of vegetable oil to ⅔ or ½ a cup

26	oz. beans, black-eyed or honey preferred
4	bouillon cubes
1	habanero pepper
2	tsp. ground nutmeg
3	tatashe (red bell) peppers, OR …
3½	cups of watery tomato puree
2	large onions
¾	cup vegetable oil
2	liters of cool or warm water

Salt (to taste)

DIRECTIONS

About three hours before cooking, soak and wash the beans to remove the coat. When the entire coat has been removed, place the beans in a bowl and add enough water to cover them. Let soak for 1-2 hours.

Wash the tatashe pepper, removing the seeds, as they tend to produce a bitter taste. Wash the habanero pepper and set aside. Cut the onions into pieces. Crush the bouillon cubes and set aside.

Blend the soaked beans, cognizant of the fact that the consistency and smoothness are a big key to the success of the recipe. Blend the beans, tatashe (or tomato puree), onions, habanero pepper, and ground nutmeg together with some of the water and pour the mix into a bowl.

Add the vegetable oil. Slowly add the remaining water and stir the mixture at the same time, blending all of the ingredients. Add salt to taste and stir very well.

Add about an inch of water to a big pot and spoon the moi moi into aluminum foil packets. Seal them and place them into the pot on low heat. Cooking times will vary based on how many packets you prepare. Cover the pot and cook for about 45 minutes to an hour. The final product should not be watery.

Let the packets cool after removing from the pot, unwrap and enjoy.

Healthy Tips:
Diabetes

WHAT IS DIABETES?

Diabetes is a disease where your body either does not make enough insulin or cannot use the insulin it makes. Insulin helps bring sugar into your body's cells for energy. Without insulin, sugars build up in your blood and can damage your eyes, nerves, and kidneys.

CAN I MANAGE MY DIABETES THROUGH MY DIET?

Yes! Having a healthy diet is one step toward managing your diabetes. Your doctor may also prescribe you medicine to manage your diabetes. A dietitian/nutritionist can help you develop a balanced diet to control your blood sugar while still including many of your favorite foods.

WHAT FOODS WILL MAKE MY BLOOD SUGAR GO UP?

Foods containing carbohydrates (carbs) will raise your blood sugar. Foods that contain a lot of carbohydrates per serving include grains (bread, rice, and pasta), starchy vegetables (potatoes, peas, and corn), fruits and fruit juices, dairy products, and sweets or desserts.

SHOULD I AVOID ALL CARBS?

No! Many high carb foods contain nutrients that give your body the energy it needs. Pick carbs that contain fiber like whole grains (whole wheat bread and pasta, brown rice, bulgur, oats, and quinoa), legumes, fruits, and vegetables. These foods also contain vitamins and minerals to support your healthy lifestyle.

ARE THERE CARBS THAT I SHOULD AVOID?

Some sources of carbs like sodas, candy, and desserts contain a lot of sugar but little nutrition. These foods are okay to eat sometimes, but most of the carbs that you eat should come from nutritious foods like whole grains, beans, vegetables, and fruits.

DOES IT MATTER WHEN I EAT?

Yes! Eating well-balanced meals and snacks throughout the day helps keep your blood sugar and insulin levels steady. Skipping meals will make it harder to manage your diabetes. Eat small, frequent meals and snacks to keep your blood sugar and energy levels in check.

SAMPLE MEAL PLANS

Foods in orange contain carbs; the number in brackets is how many servings of carbs are in that food.

MEAL PLAN 1	
BREAKFAST	1 cup cooked oatmeal [2] with 2 tbsp peanut butter, ½ large sliced banana [1], and coffee or tea with milk and artificial sweetener.
A.M. SNACK	One fruit cup packed in juice [1] and one boiled egg.
LUNCH	1 cup black bean soup [2] with ½ of a baked plantain [2] and side salad.
P.M. SNACK	6 whole wheat crackers [1] 1 oz of cheddar cheese.
DINNER	4 oz grilled or blackened fish with ½ cup braised collard greens and 1 cup brown rice [3].

MEAL PLAN 2	
BREAKFAST	Two eggs scrambled with non-starchy vegetables of your choice (try spinach, mushrooms, onions, or peppers). Serve with ½ cup of home fries [1], one large banana [2], and coffee or tea with milk and artificial sweetener.
A.M. SNACK	1 cup chopped non-starchy vegetables of your choice (try celery, carrots, and cucumber) with ⅓ cup hummus [1].
LUNCH	Sandwich with 2 slices whole grain bread [2], 2 oz lean ham, 1 slice reduced-fat cheese, sliced tomato, lettuce, ¼ avocado. Serve with 17 small pretzels [1] and ¾ cup of reduced-fat yogurt [1].
P.M. SNACK	1 banana [2] with 1 oz dry-roasted peanuts or 1 tbsp peanut butter.
DINNER	1 cup [3] spaghetti with ⅓ cup of red sauce and 2 large meatballs. Serve with steamed broccoli and/or a side salad.

SERVING SIZES FOR SOME CARBOHYDRATES

GRAINS, CEREALS & BREADS

FOOD	SERVING SIZE
Biscuit	1 (2 ½ inches across)
Ble (bulgur), cooked	½ cup
Bread	1 slice (1 oz)
Bun (hotdog or hamburger)	1 oz or ½ bun
Chapatti, small	1 (6 inches across)
Cornbread	1 (1¾ inch cube or 1½ oz)
Corn meal, uncooked	3 Tbsp
Crackers, any type	6 crackers
Grits, cooked	½ cup
Millet, cooked	⅓ cup
Oatmeal, plain, cooked	½ cup
Pancake	1 (¼ inch thick, 4 inches across)
Pasta, cooked	⅓ cup
Popcorn, popped	3 cups
Chips, regular	9-13 (¾ oz)
Pretzels	¾ oz, about 17 small twists
Rice, brown or white, cooked	⅓ cup
Rice cakes	2 (4 inches across)
Roll, plain	1 (2 ½ inches across)
Sweetened Cereals	½ cup
Tortilla, corn or flour, 6 inches across	1

FRUIT: FRESH, DRIED OR CANNED

FOOD	SERVING SIZE
Apple, unpeeled	1 (4 oz)
Applesauce, unsweetened	½ cup
Banana	½ large or 1 small (4 oz)
Berries, any type	¾ cup
Cantaloupe	1 cup cubed (11 oz)
Dried fruit (raisins, craisins, cherries)	2 tbsp
Fruit, any, canned in juice	½ cup
Fruit juice, 100% juice	½ cup
Grapefruit, fresh	½ large (11 oz)
Grapes	17 small (3 oz)
Mango, fresh	½ of a medium fruit
Orange, fresh	1 (6-7 oz)
Pineapple, fresh	¾ cup
Tangerines, small	2 (8 oz)
Watermelon	1¼ cup (13-14 oz)

STARCHY VEGETABLES

FOOD	SERVING SIZE
Baked beans	⅓ cup
Beans, any, not in sauce (black, red, lima, navy, garbanzo, pinto)	½ cup
Cassava (yuca)	⅓ cup
Corn	½ cup
Hominy (posole)	¾ cup
Lentils, all types	½ cup
Peas, black-eyed or split	½ cup
Peas, green	½ cup
Plantain, green, boiled	½ large
Plantain, sweet, fried	¼ large
Potato, baked with skin	¼ large (3 oz)
Potato, pan-fried (home fries)	½ cup
Potato, mashed with dairy	½ cup
Sweet potato (yam)	½ cup
Refried beans, canned	½ cup
Winter squash	1 cup

Living with HIV

Thanks to advances in science and medicine, people living with HIV (PLWH) can expect to live a healthy, normal and very long life.[1] This hasn't always been the case. Over 30 years ago, when the HIV epidemic was rising, the average life expectancy of a newly diagnosed PLWH was 1-2 years. Today a person diagnosed at age 20, who commences HIV medication, also known as *Antiretral Viral therapy (ARV)* can expect to live well into their seventies.[2]

ARVs are one of the most important tools for PLWH. Considering there is no "cure" for HIV at this time, daily viral suppression medication allows a PLWH's immune system to return to normal function within 6 months of starting treatment. ARVs reduce the amount of HIV virus in the blood at any given time—this is referred to as viral loads. Viral suppression is achieved when the viral load is very low, which is defined as less than 200 copies of HIV per milliliter of blood.

When a PLWH achieves viral suppression, they become "undetectable," which means that there is no discernible level of HIV virus in the system and blood tests will not detect HIV. Persons who are undetectable are also unable to transmit the HIV virus to others. This is referred as being, "untransmitable." A common expression for PLWH, who are both undetectable and untransmitable, is U=U.[3]

Achieving undetectable viral status effectively means that a PLWH has no risk of transmitting HIV to a partner who is HIV-negative, through sexual activity. Moreover, being undetectable allows mothers who are HIV-positive to give birth to a HIV-negative baby, as long as they continue to take their ARVs throughout the entire pregnancy. After giving birth, undetectable mothers can also expect to breast-feed their children without risk of transmitting the virus.[4]

Support for PLWH

Living with HIV is a journey, and help is available for PLWH for every step of it. From HIV diagnosis, to medication prescription and adherence support, and continuing with supportive referrals and individualized care and intervention, PLWH can expect to work with health care professionals who are dedicated to helping the HIV community. No one should have to go through this journey alone. Due in part to federal funding and resources dedicated to supporting PLWH, local, state and national health care institutions are committed to improving PLWH health outcomes and livelihoods.

<200

VIRAL SUPPRESSION IS ACHIEVED WHEN THE VIRAL LOAD IS VERY LOW, WHICH IS DEFINED AS LESS THAN **200 COPIES** OF HIV PER MILLILITER OF BLOOD.

U=U

UNDETECTABLE = UNTRANSMITABLE: WHEN A PLWH HAS NO DISCERNIBLE LEVEL OF HIV IN THEIR SYSTEM AND CANNOT PASS THE VIRUS ON TO OTHERS.

WHAT IS A CARE TEAM?

Every person living with HIV/AIDS is entitled to a robust, interprofessional care team. Care team professionals are focused on improving health outcomes and addressing social determinant of health (SDoH) barriers to accessing health services. A typical care team will consist of:

■ **Providers:** A Medical Doctor (MD), Nurse Practitioner (NP), Physician Assistant (PA), and/or sometimes a Registered Nurse (RN) will prescribe ARV therapy, monitor co-morbidities, and support healthy living activities to encourage positive health outcomes;

■ **RN case managers:** support ongoing health needs, including ARV adherence, viral loads, CD4 count, and other chronic health concerns, such as diabetes and hypertension. The RN case manager will support provider involvement in PLWH's care, serving as a clinical liaison for patient and provider;

■ **Medical Case Managers (MCM):** support PLWH with their social determinant of health (SDoH) needs, including transportation, financial, insurance, and childcare. MCMs also ensure that bi-annual applications for Ryan White and HIV Drug Assistance Program (HDAP) recertification's are completed in a timely manner. MCMs meet regularly with PLWH in office settings, via telehealth, and even conduct home visits and/or provide medical companionship to medical appointments;

■ **Community Health Workers (CHW):** often working in tandem with MCMs, CHWs provide additional support for PLWH with SDoH needs, such as housing, including applying for affordable and sustainable housing programs, and seeking community financial support resources to pay for back-logged rent and utility bills. They help with other miscellaneous needs, such as finding employment, education, and nutritional services (such as SNAP [Food Stamps] benefits). CHWs also support psychosocial needs, providing one-on-one counseling and making supportive referrals as needed;

■ **Integrated Behavioral Health (BH) Services:** such as therapy, counseling, group support, detox and substance use services, and/or psychiatry. These essential BH services are available for all PLWH, often upon referral from provider, RN, MCM or CHW, BH.

WHAT IS THE RYAN WHITE CARES ACT?

The Ryan White HIV/AIDS program is funded by the US Health Resources and Services Administration (HRSA) grant, which supplies states, cities, and local, community-based organizations with funding to support PLWH to improve their health outcomes and reduce the

WHAT IS A SOCIAL DETERMINANT OF HEALTH?

SOCIAL DETERMINANTS OF HEALTH (SDoH) ARE THE CONDITIONS THAT EXIST IN THE COMMUNITIES WHERE PEOPLE LIVE, WHICH HAVE DIRECT AND INDIRECT EFFECTS ON THE HEALTH, QUALITY OF LIFE, ACCESS, AND LONGEVITY OF PEOPLE.

THERE ARE 5 MAIN DOMAINS WHICH COMPRISE SDoH, INCLUDING:

■ HEALTH ACCESS AND QUALITY
■ ENVIRONMENT
■ EDUCATION
■ ECONOMIC STABILITY
■ SOCIAL AND COMMUNITY CONTEXT

ONE OF THE MAIN THINGS TO KEEP IN MIND WHEN CONSIDERING SDoH IS ACCESS – ACCESS TO HEALTHCARE, ACCESS TO EDUCATION, ACCESS TO FOOD, ACCESS TO A SAFE LIVING ENVIRONMENT. ACCESS CAN BE INTERPRETED AS LITERAL TRANSPORTATION, AND IT CAN ALSO MEAN ELIGIBILITY (SUCH AS FINANCIAL, OR ACCEPTANCE), OR QUALIFICATION, BASED ON DEMOGRAPHIC CRITERIA.

COMMON SDoH INCLUDE, BUT ARE NOT LIMITED TO:

■ HEALTH INSURANCE
■ EDUCATION
■ CHILD CARE
■ FOOD SECURITY
■ JOBS
■ TRANSPORTATION
■ HOUSING
■ UTILITIES
■ SAFETY
■ SECURITY

THERE IS ALSO THE ARGUMENT THAT STIGMA AND EXCLUSION CAN BE A SDoH. IF A PARTICULAR GROUP OF PEOPLE DO NOT ACCEPT A PERSON FOR WHO THEY ARE, INCLUDING THEIR RACE, COLOR OF THEIR SKIN, ETHNICITY, RELIGION, SEXUAL ORIENTATION, GENDER IDENTITY, OR ABILITIES, THEN THAT CAN DIRECTLY IMPACT THAT INDIVIDUAL'S ABILITY TO THRIVE (CDC, 2021).

REFERENCE
Centers for Disease Control and Prevention (CDC). (2021). What Are Social Determinants of Health [Online]. (Available from : https://www.cdc.gov/socialdeterminants/about.html (accessed: 23 April 2021).

WHO WAS RYAN WHITE?

THE RYAN WHITE HIV/AIDS PROGRAM IS NAMED AFTER 13-YEAR-OLD RYAN WHITE, WHO WAS DIAGNOSED AT AGE 13 WITH HIV, WHICH WAS DERIVED FROM A BLOOD TRANSFUSION IN 1984. HE FACED SIGNIFICANT DISCRIMINATION IN HIS COMMUNITY WHEN HE TRIED TO CONTINUE HIS EDUCATION, AND HIS FIGHT TO ATTEND SCHOOL GAINED NATIONAL ATTENTION. RYAN WHITE IS A PROMINENT NAME IN THE HIV/AIDS COMMUNITY BECAUSE DUE TO HIS ADVOCACY, AND THE ATTENTION HIS CASE RECEIVED, REGULATIONS NOW REQUIRE SCREENING OF BLOOD DONATIONS TO PREVENT HIV TRANSMISSION (HRSA, 2021).

REFERENCE
Human Resources & Services Administration (HRSA). (2021). Who was Ryan White [Online] Available at: https://hab.hrsa.gov/about-ryan-white-hivaids-program/who-was-ryan-white (accessed on 23 April 2021).

transmission of HIV in vulnerable populations.[5] Conceived in 1990, the Ryan Whites Comprehensive AIDS Resources Emergency (CARE) Act provides federal funding for community-based care to low-income individuals and families with HIV.[6] Over the past 30-years, the RW program has been renewed and reinvested in throughout many presidencies; in fiscal year 2020, $2.39 billion dollars was awarded to fund the following key programs:

■ **Part A:** covers medical and support services in areas that are disproportionately affected by HIV/AIDS, via Eligible Metropolitan Areas (EMAs) and through Transitional Grant Areas (TGAs).

■ **Part B:** available throughout all 50 US states, the District of Columbia and US territories, Part B provides funding to improve the availability, organization and quality of HIV health care and support services.

■ **Part C:** supports community-based organizations (CBOs) to provide primary health care services and support services in outpatient settings for PLWH/

■ **Part D:** supports the funding of primary and specialty medical care for women, children, infants and youth living with HIV and their affected family members in outpatient settings via CBOs.

■ **Part F:** offers clinician training and technical assistance for improving health care systems and models aimed at reducing HIV transmission and improving health outcomes for PLH via 4 specific areas:

→ **Special Projects of National Significance (SPNS) Program:** aimed at developing, reviewing and duplicating innovative strategies for HIV care and treatment for PLWH, and reduce HIV transmission among high-risk, underserved populations.

→ **AIDS Education and Training Center Program:** comprises 8 regional training centers (as well as 130 locally affiliated sites) and two national centers aimed at improving interprofessional collaboration, training and education on HIV for providers.

→ **Dental Programs:** provides comprehensive dental benefits for PLWH via the HIV/AIDS Dental Reimbursement Program and Community-Based Dental Partnership Program.

→ **Minority AIDS Initiative:** focused on improving health outcomes for PLWH, who are disproportionally affected by HIV/AIDS, such as black/African Americans, Latinx and LGBTQIA+ populations.

4
Sweets

NOW WE'RE TALKING. SATISFY YOUR SWEET TOOTH WITH CANDIED FRUIT, CARIBBEAN PASTRY, OR A HAITIAN SWEET DRINK.

Fruit Confit

The beauty of Fruit Confit, or candied fruit, is its flexibility. Our submitted recipe calls for prunes, strawberries, and grapes, but try anything you like, including pears, bananas, apples, or whatever your heart desires. The final product can be preserved in a sealed glass bottle for a long period of time.

To make this recipe healthier, you could reduce the amount of sugar, but that will likely change the texture of the finished product.

Instead, we suggest keeping this recipe as is and eating it in moderation.

Plain fruit is an easy and healthy dessert alternative

INGREDIENTS

3 cups sugar
2 cups fruits (prunes, grapes, strawberries, etc.)
2 cups water
¼ teaspoon vanilla or anise extract
1 vanilla bean
Pinch of salt

DIRECTIONS

Boil the sugar and water in a pot, reducing to about two cups.

Add fruit and simmer, partially covered, for about 30-40 minutes, until sugar dissolves.

Add vanilla or anise extract and a pinch of salt to taste. If you would like to add more vanilla flavoring, split the vanilla bean and add it to the mixture as it simmers.

Enjoy on vanilla ice cream or toast.

Fried Ripe Plantain

Plantains are available in grocery stores across New England, if playing second banana to, well, bananas. However, they are a staple food in tropical climates. In fact, they're the tenth most important staple food in the world. Together with bananas, they provide 25 percent of the caloric intake for 70 million people across Africa. Plantains are known as "cooking bananas" because they are somewhat neutral in flavor when eaten raw, and so are prepared in many ways that tend to enhance or draw out flavor. Frying plantains, for instance, tends to caramelize them. From island to island across the Caribbean, recipes vary. Try this simple start. Fry one and find out what you've been missing, and then move onto other cooking variations. And, by the way, a ripe plantain is mostly black with a little yellow coloring on it. It will still be somewhat firm when you press into it.

INGREDIENTS

1   cup of oil
2-3 ripe plantains

DIRECTIONS

Cut sides of plantains to peel (peeling a plantain can be slightly more difficult than peeling a banana). After peeling, cut into three pieces, and then cut each piece lengthwise into three, for a total of nine pieces.

Add oil to the frying pan and let it warm up on medium heat. Add plantain pieces and cook for about five minutes, until browned to your liking.

Salted Caramel Golden Pears

Don't we all deserve something like this in our lives? The sweetness and softness of this dreamy dessert can be enhanced with the simplest of sides: a scoop of vanilla ice cream. This treat can be shared with guests, or the salted caramel sauce can be frozen for future indulgences when the fancy strikes.

Cutting the sugar, butter, cream, and salt in half will result in half the amount of caramel, which will significantly lighten up this recipe and may let you enjoy the flavor of the pears even more!

INGREDIENTS

4 golden pears, washed and de-stemmed
1 cup granulated sugar
6 tbsp. salted butter, room temperature, cut into 6 pieces
½ cup heavy cream, room temperature
1 tsp. Pink Himalayan salt
Popsicle sticks or chopsticks

DIRECTIONS

Add the sugar to a small pot on medium high heat. When the sugar is almost melted, add butter and stir together.

Reduce heat to medium as the sugar becomes darker in color. Add heavy cream slowly until blended. Add Pink Himalayan salt and stir continuously until caramel is thick and creamy, reducing heat if necessary. Remove from heat.

Remove stems from pears and insert popsicle sticks or chopsticks. Dip pears in the salted caramel. Place on baking paper or parchment. Let cool and enjoy.

Caribbean Coconut Doughboy

We know that many magnificent recipes have come from the Caribbean. And we know we like doughboys in New England. Head to New Bedford and ask anybody on the street about "johnnycakes" and they will give you their favorite recipe. But it's that central word that makes this treat so special. Coconut, or coconut dough, to take it one step further, makes this bread recipe teeter between side dish and dessert, flexible enough to be enjoyed warm with butter, or to complement a main course.

INGREDIENTS

1	cup finely grated coconut
1	tsp. cinnamon
1	tsp. nutmeg
1	tsp. allspice
1½	tsp. salt
½	cup sugar
1½	lb. flour
½	cup vegetable oil or plant milk
1	tbsp. yeast
½	tsp. baking soda

DIRECTIONS

In a deep bowl (or a bread maker), combine flour, cinnamon, nutmeg, allspice, salt, and sugar. Add grated coconut, yeast, baking soda, some warm water and oil or milk. Knead for five minutes. Let dough sit for 1 to 2 minutes, and then knead for another 2 to 3 minutes until dough is smooth and springy. Cover and place in a warm area to double in size.

Preheat oven to 350. Deflate dough and shape into small cakes, or one flat bake. Allow to rest 3 to 5 minutes. Bake in a cake pan for 30 to 45 minutes, testing with a toothpick.

Pecan Strawberry French Toast

French toast is made by soaking bread in a beaten egg mixture and then pan frying it. What you do with it once it comes out of the pan is up to you. Our recipe calls for a sweet mixture of flavors building from the cinnamon-nutmeg-vanilla combination in the egg mixture, to caramelized pecans, to a sugar-frosted strawberry crescendo. What are we waiting for? Let's get to the kitchen!

INGREDIENTS

Consider reducing to ¾ cup sugar to reduce overall calories

Consider reducing to ½ stick of butter

Using whole or low-fat milk will reduce the overall fat content of this recipe

⅓	cup eggs whites or 2-4 whole eggs
1	tbsp. cinnamon
½	tbsp. nutmeg
½	tsp. of vanilla extract
1	cup sugar
⅓–½	cup pecans
1	stick butter, room temperature, cut into 6 slices
½	cup heavy cream, room temperature
4–8	strawberries
4–8	slices bread of choice
	Maple syrup, optional

DIRECTIONS

In a small bowl, mix eggs or egg whites, cinnamon, nutmeg, and vanilla extract. Whisk ingredients from edge of bowl to middle until mixture is combined. Set aside, covered, in the refrigerator.

To make the pecan topping, add the sugar to a small pot on medium high heat. When almost melted, add butter and stir. Reduce heat to medium as the sugar becomes darker in color. Add heavy cream slowly until blended. Add pecans and stir continuously until caramel is thick and creamy, reducing heat if needed while stirring. Remove from heat.

To prepare the fruit topping, slice strawberries and lightly sprinkle with sugar.

Melt butter in a skillet on medium low heat. Dip the slices of bread in the egg mixture on both sides allowing excess to drip. Drop them onto skillet, cooking both sides evenly golden brown.

Plate your French toast with caramel pecans, and strawberries on top, with or without syrup. Enjoy!

Akasan

Akasan is a beloved, thick, almost pudding-like drink, one that Haitians can buy from vendors, but mostly make at home. Our recipe calls for "Akasan powder," which is corn flour. It also calls for some creativity by you. The amount of milk and corn flour you use is up to you, depending on how thick you want your Akasan to be. Start with a half cup of each. Noyau extract is homemade almond extract; don't hesitate to buy it off the shelf.

INGREDIENTS

3–4	cups of water
3–4	cinnamon sticks
6–8	anise stars (or 2-3 tsp. anise star extract)
¼	tsp. salt
¼	cup of sugar
1	tsp. vanilla extract
1	tsp. noyau extract
1	12oz. can evaporated milk
	Akasan powder
	Milk, whole, skim or almond

Try reducing to sugar content to 3 tablespoons

Using whole milk in place of evaporated milk will also save on some fat and calories

Skim or almond milk will have significantly less fat and calories than whole milk

DIRECTIONS

Add water, salt, cinnamon sticks, and anise stars to a pot and bring to a low boil.

In a large bowl, add akasan powder and milk slowly, stirring so that the combination does not get lumpy. Add the mixture to the boiling water slowly, stirring as you go. Let it cook for about 15 minutes. Then, add sugar, vanilla extract, noyau extract and evaporated milk slowly.

Akasan can be served warm, but is arguably better chilled on a nice warm summer, tropical-like day.

Healthy Tips: Healthy Plate

MY PLATE PLANNER

The Plate Method is a simple way to plan meals. You don't need to count anything or read a long list of foods. All you need is a 9-inch plate. The Healthy Plate is a simple and effective way to eat balanced, healthy meals.

WHAT IS THE HEALTHY PLATE?

The Plate Method divides your plate into halves and quarters.

- **½ vegetables.** This gives you plenty of water and fiber to fill you up (plus, they have lots of healthy vitamins and minerals). You can fill half your plate with more than one vegetable so you won't get tired of your favorites.
- **¼ starch.** This ensures you get enough energy without overdoing it. Some vegetables are higher in starch (corn, peas, yams), and belong on this part of the plate.
- **¼ protein.** Like the starch, you'll get enough protein without overdoing it. Bake, broil, boil or steam your protein instead of frying. Low-fat proteins are better for your heart and waistline.

TRICK YOUR EYES

The Healthy Plate is only 9 inches in diameter. A typical dinner plate is 11-12 inches. Eating off of a smaller plate can trick your eyes into thinking you're getting more food and leave you feeling satisfied with less.

THE PERFECT DRINK

All the plates are served with water — the perfect zero-calorie beverage. Staying away from juices, sodas, and other caloric beverages helps limit your overall energy intake and keeps you from having excess sugar. It also frees up your calorie budget for FOOD, which offers more nutrition.

CULTURALLY COMPETENT

The Healthy Plate works with all sorts of cultural preferences and lets you pick and choose the veggies, starches, and proteins you prefer.

REFERENCE

My Plate Planner content courtesy of the New York City Department of Health and Mental Hygiene.

THE PLATE METHOD

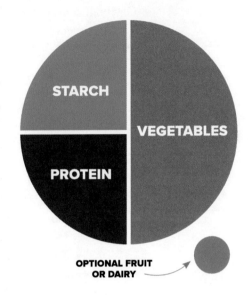

OPTIONAL FRUIT OR DAIRY

PORTION SIZES

Learn how to plan your meal.

1 STARCH = 1 CUP

- COLD CEREAL, BREAD, BROWN RICE, POTATOES, CORN, PEAS, YAMS, OATMEAL

2 OR MORE VEGETABLES = 2 CUPS

- BROCCOLI, LETTUCE, OKRA, CARROTS, GREEN BEANS, SPINACH, CABBAGE

1 PROTEIN = 4 OUNCES

- BEEF, CHICKEN, FISH, BEANS, NUTS, EGG

1 FRUIT OR 1 DAIRY = 1 SMALL PIECE OR 1 CUP

- APPLE, ORANGE, BANANA, 1% MILK, YOGURT

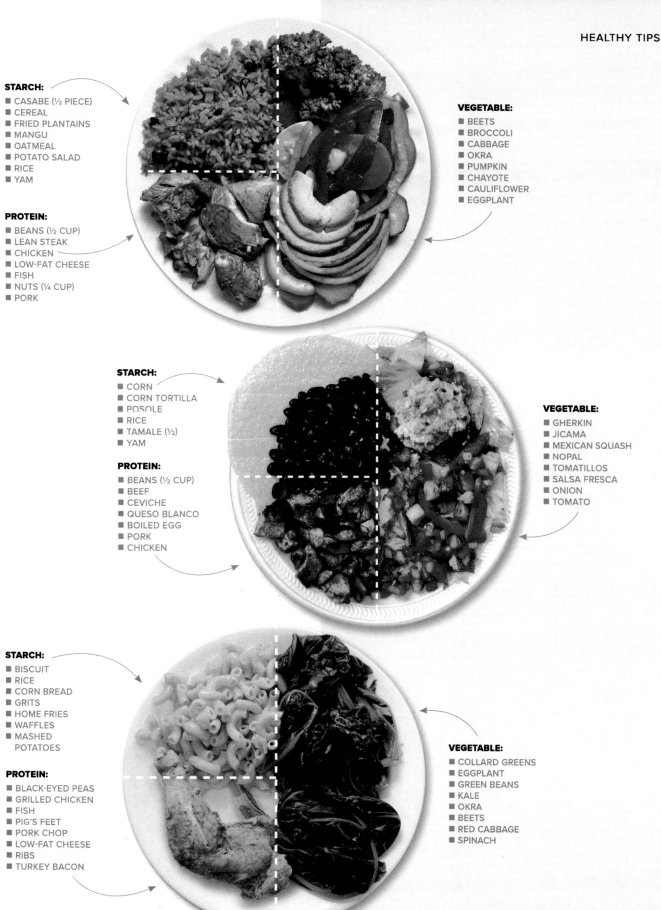

STARCH:
- CASABE (½ PIECE)
- CEREAL
- FRIED PLANTAINS
- MANGU
- OATMEAL
- POTATO SALAD
- RICE
- YAM

PROTEIN:
- BEANS (½ CUP)
- LEAN STEAK
- CHICKEN
- LOW-FAT CHEESE
- FISH
- NUTS (¼ CUP)
- PORK

VEGETABLE:
- BEETS
- BROCCOLI
- CABBAGE
- OKRA
- PUMPKIN
- CHAYOTE
- CAULIFLOWER
- EGGPLANT

STARCH:
- CORN
- CORN TORTILLA
- POSOLE
- RICE
- TAMALE (½)
- YAM

PROTEIN:
- BEANS (½ CUP)
- BEEF
- CEVICHE
- QUESO BLANCO
- BOILED EGG
- PORK
- CHICKEN

VEGETABLE:
- GHERKIN
- JICAMA
- MEXICAN SQUASH
- NOPAL
- TOMATILLOS
- SALSA FRESCA
- ONION
- TOMATO

STARCH:
- BISCUIT
- RICE
- CORN BREAD
- GRITS
- HOME FRIES
- WAFFLES
- MASHED POTATOES

PROTEIN:
- BLACK-EYED PEAS
- GRILLED CHICKEN
- FISH
- PIG'S FEET
- PORK CHOP
- LOW-FAT CHEESE
- RIBS
- TURKEY BACON

VEGETABLE:
- COLLARD GREENS
- EGGPLANT
- GREEN BEANS
- KALE
- OKRA
- BEETS
- RED CABBAGE
- SPINACH

Food is fuel

One of the themes we've talked about in this book is that food is a reason to come to the table, to connect with family and friends, and to stop — if even for a few moments — and be present. It may seem that as our days become busier and busier with tasks and responsibilities, finding time to sit down and share a meal may be the last thing on our agendas. Though being busy is exactly the reason that we should intentionally carve out some time to eat, together.

Studies show that family bonds are strengthened when meals are shared together, and a sense of connectedness and protection results from the time spent together. Moreover, eating together, in a communal manner, helps lower risks of mental health issues, including isolation and depression, and reduces negative health outcomes, such as alcohol and substance use (CDC, 2021).

In many cultures, there is a tradition of a weekly family dinner, which allows families to schedule a set time each week to reunite at the dinner table. This is a tradition that transcends communities and national borders — it is a human desire to find connection in our community, as a means of survival, as a means of happiness. In the Scandinavian cultures, there is a term called, *hygge,* which is a Dutch term that means "quality of cosiness and comfortable conviviality that engenders a feeling of contentment or well-being" (Altam, 2016). Hygge can be interpreted broadly, though one of the common themes is to find time to connect with

people you enjoy spending time with, because it brings you joy. Eating together is a simple way to evoke this feeling, and carving time out each week to make it a routine will lend positive, healthy outcomes for everyone included.

There are a number of organizations in the Boston communities that offer meals to community members, such as *Community Servings* (they have medically-tailored meals that are delivered to eligible patient's homes), which is based in Jamaica Plain, and started off as a meal-delivery service for PLWH. Another agency, *Boston Living Center,* offers breakfast and lunch throughout the week at their site for PLWH. They also have cooking classes and workshops, and offer nutritional consultations.

Many more places exist for PLWH and persons in need of a warm meal and a seat at the table; feel free to ask your provider or care team representative for more information on places to eat, and to connect with your community.

However you define community, know that the beauty of being alive means that you have the choice to choose with whom you'd like to share your time, your meals. Family and community dinners can be an opportunity to meet new people, or reconnect with friends and loved ones. In the spirit of breaking bread, remember that when you sit at the table together, you are choosing to celebrate life.

GET IN TOUCH

- **COMMUNITY SERVINGS**
  179 AMORY ST.,
  JAMAICA PLAIN,
  MA 02130
  (617) 522-7777
  www.servings.org

- **BOSTON LIVING CENTER**
  29 STANHOPE ST.,
  BOSTON, MA 02116
  (617) 236-1012
  www.vpi.org/boston

REFERENCE

Centers for Disease Control and Prevention (CDC) (2021). Healthy Behavioral Development Starts at the Dinner Table [Online]. Available from: https://www.cdc.gov/publichealthgateway/field-notes/2019/ky-dinner-table.html (Accessed: 06 May 2021).

Altman, A. (2016, December 18). The Year of Hygge, The Danish Obsession with Getting Cozy. The New Yorker. Available from: https://newyorker.com/culture/culture-desk/the-year-of-hygge-the-danish-obsession-with-getting-cozy (Accessed: 06 May 2021).

EDITOR'S NOTE:

We are pleased (and privileged) to share some sentiments, including testimonials and poems, from some of the PLWH we serve in our communities. They have provided some key insight, words of advice, encouragement, and real talk about what it is like to live with HIV. They are brave and their words are beautiful. We are grateful for their contributions.

'I know I will be OK.'

I found out I was HIV+ three days after graduating college. It was a shock but not a surprise; I had the common "super flu" that hits people when they seroconvert from HIV- to HIV+. I was 24 years old, and two weeks later I moved to the Bay Area, California, to start my career as a middle school math and science teacher.

I was lucky in many ways; I moved to a state that was very queer-friendly and very HIV-knowledgeable. I found a social worker who immediately helped me get on meds and hooked me up with the greatest and nicest nurses. I felt seen, accommodated, and respectfully serviced as a trans/non-binary Asian person. It took me less than a month to become undetectable since I'm very on top of my meds.

I call it luck, but I can also call it privilege that I was able to easily access necessary health care. I didn't have family or friends when I moved to California I just had the backbone and adventure spirit to not only survive but thrive. I had the kind of spirit where I can be dropped in the middle of a foreign country and still find my way around.

I know that HIV care looked very different and scary 30 years ago. Medication used to consist of multiple pills and doctor's visits, but nowadays it's just one pill and quarterly check-ups. Some HIV+ patients even live longer than HIV- people simply because we stay on our meds and get checked up with doctors more often. We know a lot more about HIV now than we did not even one generation ago.

Although there is not a cure yet, I know I will be ok. It is now just the stigma of HIV that I live with and fight every day. It is my belief that it is our duty to fight for better healthcare, the kind that our ancestors could not have when they were alive. And so that the legacy we leave the youth in our community is healthy, safe, and accepting. This starts with talking about HIV.

Thank you for reading my story.

If I Could Cure the World

If I could cure the world, Nobody would care. It never be enough

To be taken seriously, Feel I'm not enough,
   Like a old coat ripped, Beaten down and torn

Only reason I'm still around, Be used abused and worn,
Like dirty boots kicked to the ground

I fall for the fake games and lies told,
   I should know this by now being this old

Searching for love is said to be bad,
   Not giving it a try will I know it could be had

Is it my destiny to be so alone? Last number in the black book,
   Fail safe when nothing comes thru. Could I ever be your first look?
   Reliability through and through

Is that too much to ask? Is it that hard of a task?

Double standard, All goose no gander. Mornings to afternoons,
   evenings to good nights. My texts unanswered,
   calls ring till voicemail light

Raggedy Andie under the bed gusty. No wonder I feel dusty and rusty

I've started to push people further away,
   In hopes of my own brighter day

Who am I kidding? No matter what I do,
   No one will ever accept you for you

If I could cure the world, Nobody would care, It never be enough,
   Be true to yourself, don't ever give up.

Every Bite

With every breath inhale the good.

With every exhale blow out the bad.

With every bite
   taste the comfortable sweet.

With every swallow
   may your tummy enjoy the treat.

When you repeat your worries retreat.

Remember every bite
   all the way to the fin.

When you finally get there —
   Wait For iiiiiiiit ... Do it again.

Who am I: See me, hear me, don't judge me

I thought long and hard over the past 17 years how my life has gone, about choices I have made and choices that were made for me. As a Black woman, I am thought to be someone who is always strong, capable, nurturing and thought to make the right choices in my life. But unfortunately, one fateful day in January 2004, someone made a choice for me, without asking me. I am HIV positive.

There is a lot of stigma in the Black community about HIV/AIDS that we don't talk about as a people, a community — be it African American, Caribbean, Asian or Latino/a. I don't mean any disrespect by not mentioning the Caucasian population, but I don't know how to express their thoughts or feelings about HIV/AIDS; I can only speak as a Black woman.

My growing up in Boston was good; I had great parents that supported me, directed me, guided me. With the help of my mom, I was able to pursue a college degree, and I had over 25 years of experience working in a field helping others. During that time, I was blessed to have two wonderful children — a daughter and a son — and I am very proud to be their mom.

One fateful day, I decided to start a new relationship with someone, and that person made a choice for me. I have become HIV positive because of the choice that was made for me. Please don't judge me; see me, hear me, don't judge. There is more to me than just my HIV status.

I have learned to forgive the person that caused this disease to invade my body and change it forever. I have great medical care through my clinic, and a very supportive doctor who has seen me through my journey. I am very grateful to this day.

The biggest thing that I share that I am not worthy of now is love and support because of my HIV status; I feel damaged and not the full woman that I used to be. But the biggest thing that I try to ask for from friends and family, when they are willing, is "Can I have a hug?" Giving a person a hug, who is HIV positive, you cannot catch the disease from me. It doesn't cost anyone anything other than time. If you truly love your friends and family, it is important to give hugs, if nothing more, and you cannot give kind words.

I hope that as this year goes on, and we reach the next anniversary of the National HIV/AIDS days, if anyone reads this story, please know that there are many people out there around you, who may be HIV positive and you may never know it. And they can be much more to you, if you just give us a chance. Remember what I said throughout this whole testimony: having The Virus can be a lonely journey if we choose that we cannot trust others around us. But let us be willing to change that outcome for those around us, regardless of their race or ethnicity. Try to envision that a person like me has the right to be loved, cared for, supported and encouraged. Even though I have what I have, it is only a part of me, it is not the whole of me.

Do you see me, hear me, or would you judge me if you knew who I am?

When I'm Not Here

When I'm not around, for your ridicule,
   I just stepped out, from your guilty rule.

Shampooed many years, for love from you.
   Now it seems it's time to rinse it through.

When I'm not here, not here tomorrow,
   Don't look for me the next day, I'm dead from
   the sorrow, When I'm not here, here tomorrow

Will you still love me, Or am I to borrow?
   Life comes at you hard, you got to swallow.
   Got me sideways and twisted, No fail or follow

Recollect and recall, The love that I offered
   It be the last time, My hearts your unsub

When I'm not here, not here tomorrow,
   Don't look for me the next day, I'm dead from
   the sorrow, When i'm not here, here tomorrow

Will you still love me, Or am i to borrow?
   Time will tell. I'll find out tomorrow

Cold Shoulder

Cold shoulder, warm hand
   It can be hard to understand

I'm me, you're you
   We're all we can demand

Equal to from no minus or divide
   Add to multiply by color blind coincide

Food is the way to the soul,
   No matter young or old

May all the colors we see
   Be the food we all need

Inequality clouds needs to flee
   Before we can sow equality seed

With every stir,
let your love and energy
flow into the food.

Even if you're alone,
show yourself some love.

Cook with love.
Eat with Happiness.

Healthy Tips: Eating better on a budget

GET THE MOST FOR YOUR BUDGET!

There are many ways to save money on the foods that you eat. The three main steps are planning before you shop, purchasing the items at the best price, and preparing meals that stretch your food dollars.

REFERENCE

Reprinted from Center for Nutrition Policy and Promotion, published by the United States Department of Agriculture. Part of the "10 Tips" Nutrition Education Series and based on the Dietary Guidelines for Americans. November 2011. Revised October 2016.

5 BUY IN SEASON. BUYING FRUITS AND VEGETABLES IN SEASON CAN LOWER THE COST AND ADD TO THE FRESHNESS! IF YOU ARE NOT GOING TO USE THEM ALL RIGHT AWAY, BUY SOME THAT STILL NEED TIME TO RIPEN.

6 CONVENIENCE COSTS … GO BACK TO BASICS. CONVENIENCE FOODS LIKE FROZEN DINNERS, PRE-CUT FRUITS AND VEGETABLES, AND TAKE-OUT MEALS CAN OFTEN COST MORE THAN IF YOU WERE TO MAKE THEM AT HOME. TAKE THE TIME TO PREPARE YOUR OWN—AND SAVE!

7 EASY ON YOUR WALLET. CERTAIN FOODS ARE TYPICALLY LOW-COST OPTIONS ALL YEAR ROUND. TRY BEANS FOR A LESS EXPENSIVE PROTEIN FOOD. FOR VEGETABLES, BUY CABBAGE, SWEET POTATOES, OR LOW-SODIUM CANNED TOMATOES. AS FOR FRUITS, APPLES AND BANANAS ARE GOOD CHOICES.

8 COOK ONCE … EAT ALL WEEK. PREPARE A LARGE BATCH OF FAVORITE RECIPES ON YOUR DAY OFF (DOUBLE OR TRIPLE THE RECIPE). FREEZE IN INDIVIDUAL CONTAINERS. USE THEM THROUGHOUT THE WEEK AND YOU WON'T HAVE TO SPEND MONEY ON TAKE-OUT MEALS.

1 PLAN, PLAN, PLAN! BEFORE YOU HEAD TO THE GROCERY STORE, MAKE A LIST AND PLAN YOUR MEALS FOR THE WEEK. INCLUDE MEALS LIKE STEWS, CASSEROLES, OR SOUPS, WHICH "STRETCH" EXPENSIVE ITEMS INTO MORE PORTIONS.

2 GET THE BEST PRICE. CHECK THE LOCAL NEWSPAPER, ONLINE, AND AT THE STORE FOR SALES AND COUPONS. ASK ABOUT A LOYALTY CARD FOR EXTRA SAVINGS AT STORES WHERE YOU SHOP. LOOK FOR SPECIALS OR SALES ON MEAT AND SEAFOOD—OFTEN THE MOST EXPENSIVE ITEMS ON YOUR LIST.

3 COMPARE AND CONTRAST. LOCATE THE "UNIT PRICE" ON THE SHELF DIRECTLY BELOW THE PRODUCT. USE IT TO COMPARE DIFFERENT BRANDS AND DIFFERENT SIZES OF THE SAME BRAND TO DETERMINE WHICH IS THE BEST BUY.

4 BUY IN BULK. IT IS ALMOST ALWAYS CHEAPER TO BUY FOODS IN BULK. SMART CHOICES ARE LARGE CONTAINERS OF LOW-FAT YOGURT AND LARGE BAGS OF FROZEN VEGETABLES. BEFORE YOU SHOP, REMEMBER TO CHECK IF YOU HAVE ENOUGH FREEZER SPACE.

9 GET CREATIVE WITH LEFTOVERS. SPICE UP YOUR LEFTOVERS—USE THEM IN NEW WAYS. FOR EXAMPLE, TRY LEFTOVER CHICKEN IN A STIR-FRY, OVER A GARDEN SALAD, OR IN CHILI. REMEMBER, THROWING AWAY FOOD IS THROWING AWAY YOUR MONEY!

10 EATING OUT. RESTAURANTS CAN BE EXPENSIVE. SAVE MONEY BY GETTING THE EARLY BIRD SPECIAL, GOING OUT FOR LUNCH INSTEAD OF DINNER, OR LOOKING FOR "2 FOR 1" DEALS. ASK FOR WATER INSTEAD OF ORDERING OTHER BEVERAGES, WHICH ADD TO THE BILL.

Paying tribute

Before we part, we would be remiss if we did not pay tribute to those in our communities, and across the country, who have paved the path we are all on today in the fight to raise awareness for HIV/AIDS. These individuals, among many, have raised their voices to seek acceptance for the LGBTQIA+ communities, to reduce stigma, increase access to essential medical and sexual health services, and to make it a little bit easier for people living with, and those at risk of, HIV/AIDS to be able to live the lives they deserve to live. To our national HIV/AIDS advocates, to our LGBTQIA+ trailblazers, to our local heroes, to our community partners, and beyond: We thank you!

"We're still here. We still matter. We deserve love. The virus is not going anywhere. We have youth getting [HIV] and it hits close to home."

— (ANONYMOUS) CAB MEMBER

HIV/AIDS ADVOCATES

- **George W. Bush**
  (President's Emergency Plan For AIDS Relief — PEPFAR)
- **Jahaira Dealto**
  (National Transgender Activist)
- **Dr. Anthony Fauci**
  (National Institutes of Health)
- **Twiggy Pucci Garçon**
  (Worldwide Underground Subculture Ballroom)
- **Bill Gates**
  (Co-founder, The Bill and Melinda Gates Foundation)
- **Tabytha Gonzalez**
  (Housing Works of New York)
- **Marsha P. Johnson (aka Ms. Major)**
  (Co-founder, Gay Liberation Front; advocate, prominent figure of Stonewall uprising, drag-queen, transgender, and sex worker advocate)
- **Cleve Jones**
  (Founder, AIDS Memorial Quilt)
- **Larry Kramer**
  (Act Up and Gay Men's Health Crisis Center of New York)
- **Pepper LaBeija**
  (Drag queen, icon and "the last remaining queen of the Harlem drag balls")
- **Harvey Milk**
  (Former Member of the San Francisco Board of Supervisors, LGBT advocate)
- **Ryan White**

"I am the mother who raised the children whose rainbows sparkled too brightly."

"My objective is to heal my community through trauma informed care and motivation, reminding them that they're valued, they're loved and their lives matter."

"A movement that seeks to advance only its own members is going to accomplish little."

"Once you have dialogue starting, you know you can break down prejudice."

LOCAL HEROES

- **Codman Square Health Center Consumer Advisory Board (2021)**
- **Michelle Bordeau** (Fenway Health)
- **Chastity Bowick** (Transgender Emergency Fund of Massachusetts)
- **Jen Brody** (Boston Health Care for the Homeless)
- **Gary Daffin** (Multicultural AIDS Coalition)
- **Amir Dixon** (Amir Now, INC)
- **Catrina Cooley Flag** (Multicultural AIDS Coalition)
- **Dawn Fukuda** (Mass. Department of Public Health)
- **John Gatto** (Justice Resource Institute)
- **Indigo** (Taaliyah Aiyana-Nicole Jackson) (Boston Transgender Activist)
- **Irvienne Goldson** (Action for Boston Community Development)
- **Jennease Hyatt** (Gilead Sciences)
- **Malkia Kendricks** (Women Connecting Affecting Change)
- **Larry Kessler** (AIDS Action of Massachusetts)
- **Emerson Miller** (Upham's Corner Health Center)
- **Bisola Ojikutu, MD, MPH** (Massachusetts General Hospital)
- **Jonathan Pincus, MD** (Codman Square Health Center)
- **Kamar Porter** (Justice Resource Institute)
- **Athena Vaughan** (Transgender Emergency Fund of Massachusetts)
- **Kurtis Washington** (Justice Resource Institute)

COMMUNITY PARTNERS

- ABCD (Action for Boston Community Development)
- AIDS Action Committee
- BAGLY: Boston Alliance of Gay, Lesbian, Bisexual and Transgender Youth
- Boston GLASS
- Boston Health Care for the Homeless
- Boston Living Center
- Boston Public Health Commission
- Boston Urban Pride
- Codman Academy Charter Public School
- Community Servings
- Fenway Health
- Justice Resource Institute
- Mass. Department of Public Health
- Men of Melanin Magic
- Multicultural AIDS Coalition
- NEAETC (New England AIDS Education and Training Center)
- Partners in Sex Education
- Victory Programs

"Figure it out!"

"I think the biggest impact for me would be eliminating stigma. Folks who might be HIV positive, because of what they've experienced, because of what they may have learned before having a diagnosis, it really isolates people, and we want to reduce stigma. It's the stigma that's even causing people to not do things like testing ... So I think stigma is the biggest thing that we want to relieve in the community ..."

"It's time for LGBTQ Black excellence to lead itself. We have given the power and it's time we do what needs to be done with it."

NOTES

FOREWARD
[1] Centers for Disease Control and Prevention (CDC). (2021). Community-Centered Health Home: Life on the Other Side of the Wall. [ONLINE] Available at: https://www.cdc.gov/pcd/issues/2018/17_0510.htm. [Accessed 25 March 2021].

[2] The Greater Boston Food Bank. (2021). New Projections for Eastern Mass. Show 59% Increase in Food Insecurity. [ONLINE] Available at: https://www.gbfb.org/news/press-releases/feeding-america-projections-show-increase-in-food-insecurity/. [Accessed 25 March 2021].

[3] This stat is for a person diagnosed with HIV at age 20. Comparatively, the average lifespan for a person without HIV is approximately 79 years. Additionally, a person who is diagnosed with HIV at age 20, and declines HIV medication, has a life expectancy of about 32 years. Centers for Disease Control and Prevention (CDC). (2014). HIV Care Saves Lives Infographic. [Online] Available at: www.cdc.gov/vitalsigns/hiv-aids-medical-care/infographic.html (Accessed: 25 March 2021).

[4] Health Resources & Services Administration (HRSA) (2019). Ryan White HIV/AIDS Program Legislation. [Online]. Available at: https://hab.hrsa.gov/about-ryan-white-hivaids-program/ryan-white-hivaids-program-legislation (Accessed: 25 March 2021).

[5] Evidence suggests that the first confirmed case of HIV/AIDS was in 1969, and then in the 1980's the CDC declared HIV/AIDS an epidemic. New York Times (1987). Boy's 1969 Death Suggests AIDS Invaded U.S. Several Times [Online]. Available at: https://www.nytimes.com/1987/10/28/us/boy-s-1969-death-suggests-aids-invaded-us-several-times.html (Accessed: 25 March 2021).

[6] Developed in 1987 as "an artistic expression of defiance" against HIV/AIDS, the quilt contains over 50,000 individualized, handmade, 3x6' cloth panels that use colors, names and pictures to reference the individuals lost to HIV/AIDS. AIDS Memorial (2021). The History of the Quilt. [Online]. Available at: https://www.aidsmemorial.org/quilt-history (Accessed: 25 March 2021).

[7] Created in 2015, in partnership with the National AIDS Memorial and the HIV Story Project, the Surviving Voices initiative is a longitudinal project aimed at sharing the stories and lessons from PLWH regarding their unique experiences with HIV/AIDS. It began in 2015 with the San Francisco Leather Community & AIDS; followed in 2016 by the National Hemophilia Community & AIDS; then in 2017 it focused on Women & AIDS; in 2018, Asians and Pacific Islanders (A&PIs) Community & AIDS, and most recently in 2019, the Transgender Community & AIDS. AIDS Memorial (2021). Surviving Voices [Online]. Available at: https://www.aidsmemorial.org/surviving-voices (Accessed on 25 March 2021).

[8] AIDS Coalition to Unleash Power (ACT UP) is a regional group that was developed in 1987, to unite individuals that are committed to responding to and challenging the system to raise political and cultural awareness to end the HIV/AIDS epidemic. ACTUPNY (2021). AIDS Coalition to Unleash Power. [Online]. (Available at: https://actupny.org/ (Accessed: 25 March 2021).

CHAPTER 1: AN INTRODUCTION TO HIV/AIDS
[1] PLWH can take medications, called Antiretrovirals, which will reduce HIV viral loads and support healthy living.

CHAPTER 3: LIVING WITH HIV
[1] HIV.gov (2021). Aging with HIV [Online]. Available at: https://www.hiv.gov/hiv-basics/living-well-with hiv/taking-care-of-yourself/aging-with-hiv (accessed: 18 April 2021).

[2] Centers for Disease Control and Prevention (CDC). (2021). HIV Vital Signs HIV [Online]. Available at: https://www.cdc.gov/vitalsigns/hiv-aids-medical-care/infographic.html#:~:text=HIV%20Medicines%20Help%20People%20with,HIV%20medicines%20is%2032%20years. (accessed: 18 April 2021).

[3] Centers for Disease Control and Prevention (CDC). (2021). HIV Treatment [Online]. Available at: https://www.cdc.gov/vitalsigns/hiv-aids-medical-care/infographic.html#:~:text=HIV%20Medicines%20Help%20People%20with,HIV%20medicines%20is%2032%20years. (accessed: 18 April 2021).

[4] Centers for Disease Control and Prevention (CDC). (2021). HIV: Protecting Others [Online]. Available at: https://www.cdc.gov/hiv/basics/livingwithhiv/protecting-others.html. (accessed: 18 April 2021).

[5] HIV/AIDS Bureau. (2021). About the Ryan White HIV/AIDS Program [Online]. Available at: https://hab.hrsa.gov/about-ryan-white-hivaids-program/about-ryan-white-hivaids-program (accessed: 18 April 2021).

[6] Ryan White Services Division (RWSD). (2021). Ryan White Services Division [Online]. Available at: https://www.bphc.org/whatwedo/infectious-diseases/Ryan-White-Services-Division/Pages/Ryan-White-Services-Division.aspx (accessed: 18 April 2021).

Made in the USA
Middletown, DE
06 July 2021